Creative
Knitting and
Crocheting

Creative Knitting and Crocheting

by
Rosalin
Carlson

Hearthside Press Inc.
New York

To everyone from whom I've learned anything,
and to my three sons,
Royce, Rick and little Randy,
who've helped in so many ways.

ACKNOWLEDGMENTS

Special thanks go to Anita Hames, who did the beautiful, detailed illustrations for the bulk of this book; to my husband, Richard Carlson, for making all of the diagrams, and to Rae Fiedler, who contributed the drawings for the "Designer's Boutique" section.

CONTENTS

INTRODUCTION

Even fashion has its fashions. During some epochs, the entire emphasis is on line, or style; during others, the mood of mode seems to swing to design, texture, and color—three fashion facets that are particularly important to today's woman. All three are brought into play through hand knitting (and its auxiliary, crocheting), the craft that above all others permits the fashion-conscious woman to experiment. The designing and creating of knitted couture entails a unique union of fabric and fashion design and handicraft—of the aesthetic with the creatively practical.

In this book are combined, for the first time (at least to my knowledge), all of the elements of hand-knitted fashion design. My purpose is to present to you, within these covers, all of the data and techniques you need to improvise on, or make changes in, instructions already in existence, and to design your own knits as well.

We start at the very beginning. Elementary and professional techniques are illustrated with clear, explicit drawings, so that, if you are a novice, you can take yarn and needle in hand and master the basics.

Starting with the first knitting stitch and concluding with the last item of crocheted trim, I've used the sampler method. The samplers are numbered consecutively for easy reference. You can work out each stitch or technique according to the sampler instructions, and incorporate them into your own notebook. So, at the same time that you are collecting a definitive series of patterns, stitches and techniques, you are following the kind of instruction that gives you the practice needed to read *any* kind of knitting pattern. When you're ready to design, you can make use of your notebook; the more techniques and information at your immediate disposal, the more creative you're prepared to be. Your knitted samples can be experimented with, arranged and rearranged, tried in combination—which stitch with what trim? etc.—so as to serve as idea stimulators. As you work the samplers, don't hesitate to make sketches of how you might want to use these various stitches, trims, finishes etc. in your own designs. With knitting, as with anything else, many an inspired idea gets forever lost in the shuffle because it hasn't been recorded in some way. So keep an "idea file" of fashion clippings that appeal to you, along with your own sketches; coordinate them in as many ways as strike your designing fancy.

Parts I and II give you the needed background in shaping, finishing, texture, color, and various trims. Practice in these techniques will improve your knitting in general; it will also stand you in good stead when you come to exercise your designing talents in Parts III and IV, "Basic Knitting Pattern Projects" and "Charting and Designing." The special supplement, Part V, introduces a section on how to knit according to sewing patterns that hasn't previously been included in any book of this kind.

So gather together your knitting needles, yarn, paper and pencil. Book in hand, you're ready to go, with my fervent good wishes. I hope you find the fun of being your own designer as rewarding as I have.

PART I:
BASICS OF KNITTING AND CROCHETING

GLOSSARY OF TERMS
AND ABBREVIATIONS

KNITTING TERMS:

CC — Contrasting Color
dec — Decrease
inc — Increase
K — Knit
P — Purl
psso — Pass slip stitch over knit stitch
rnd — Round
sl — Slip, or slipped
st(s) — Stitch or stitches
tog — Together
MC — Main Color
YO — Yarn Over
* — Asterisk means to continue the row repeating from the asterisk, or between asterisks if there are asterisks at the beginning and end of a portion of instructions.

CROCHETING TERMS:

ch — Chain
hdc — Half Double Crochet
dc — Double Crochet
sc — Single Crochet
sl st — Crocheted chain through knitted or crocheted material.
sp — Space
trc — Treble Crochet

STITCH GAUGE

1. Before beginning a knit of any kind, make a sampler of the pattern stitch, with the yarn and size needle you plan to use. This is in order to determine the *stitch gauge,* that is, how many stitches there are per inch. Stitches make inches, so this is essential. Therefore:

2. Measure over an area of several inches, not just one. Reason: you might miss a fractional difference which, if it were extended over several inches, could cause serious error. For example, if your knit is to measure 40 inches around, and you're off a half-stitch for each inch, you'll end up with an ultimate difference of 20 stitches. And, if your gauge is 5 stitches to 1 inch, your knit could turn out 4 inches too big or too small. Slightly fatal.

3. Let's assume you have too many stitches per inch. Solution: use a larger needle. And, if you've too few, use a smaller needle.

4. Wash your sampler and let it dry, just as you would a finished knit. See what happens. Is it colorfast? Does it stretch? Does it shrink? Better to know now, and either discard the yarn entirely, or make the appropriate allowance in your calculations.

Fig. 1 (opposite) Suggested equipment for working samplers. *A.* Double-pointed needles, size 5, 6, 7, or 8, *B.* Crochet hook, size 00, *C.* Cable stitch holder, *D.* Yarn bobbins, 1 set, *E.* Stitch holder, *F.* Yarn needle, *G.* Scissors, *H.* Tape measure, *I.* No. 8 knitting needles, straight.

1 KNITTING BASICS (FOR PRACTICE, BEFORE STARTING THE SAMPLERS)

If you are a beginner, you will want to practice these basics before starting the first sampler. Use 20 stitches for practice.

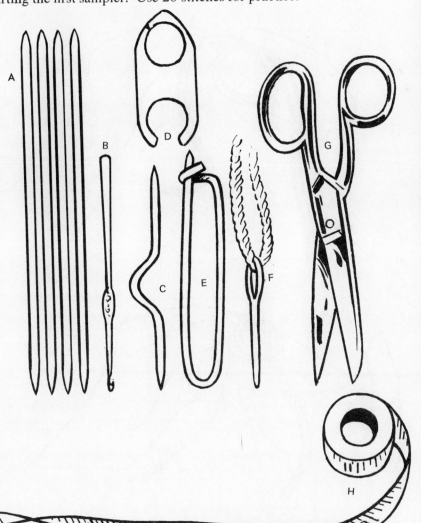

CASTING ON

a. Knitted-on Method

This is the easiest method for beginners to learn and remember, because it is very much like knitting itself.

Make a slip knot by looping the yarn in a circle, leaving a 4-inch to 6-inch end (fig. 2). Pull a loop out from underneath the center of the circle (fig. 3), place on one of the needles, and tighten. This becomes your first stitch (fig. 4).

Hold the needle with the slip knot in your left hand. Insert needle in right hand through the slip knot in the same direction as the left needle, needles crossed and ends spread apart (fig. 5). With your right

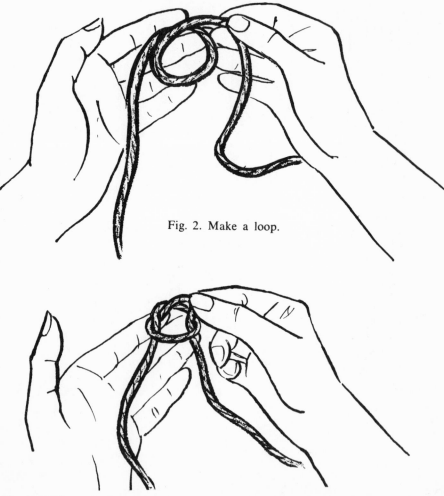

Fig. 2. Make a loop.

Fig. 3. Make a slip knot by pulling a new loop through center of first loop.

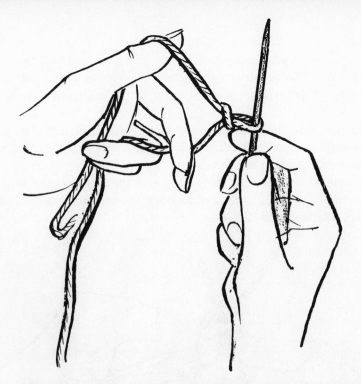

Fig. 4. Place this new loop on the knitting needle and tighten.

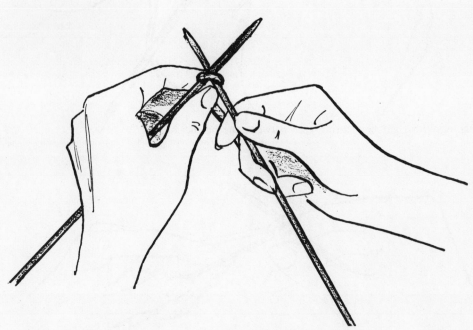

Fig. 5. Hold needle with loop in left hand and insert right-hand needle through same stitch and under left needle.

21

hand bring the yarn between the needles (fig. 6) and with the tip of the right needle force out a new loop through the slip knot (fig. 7). Stretch out this new loop a little bit and add it to the loop already on the left needle, then tighten (fig. 8). Repeat, adding on new loops until you have the required number of stitches. If later on you find your cast-on leaves an edge which is a little too loose, try turning each new loop before adding it on.

Another variation for this cast-on method is to insert the needle *between* the stitches instead of through the center of each stitch. This makes a firmer edge (fig. 9).

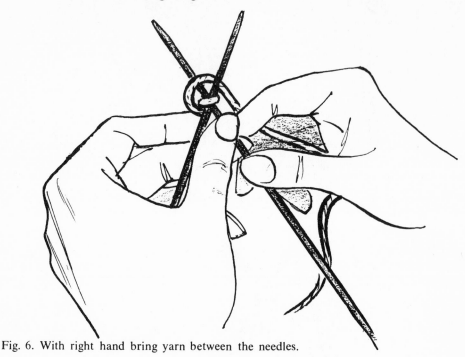

Fig. 6. With right hand bring yarn between the needles.

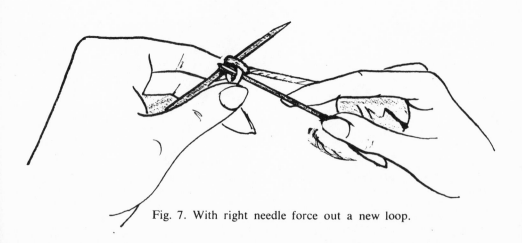

Fig. 7. With right needle force out a new loop.

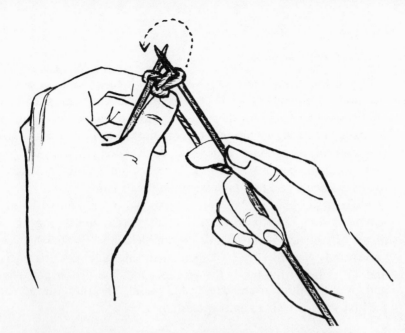

Fig. 8. Stretch it out and add it on (repeat from fig. 5 through 8
until desired number of stitches have been cast on).

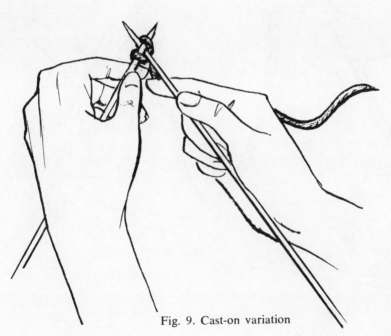

Fig. 9. Cast-on variation

b. One-Needle Method

If you are a beginner, stay with the knitted-on method and try the one-needle method later. If you have some knitting experience you will know that with this method you have to judge how long an end to leave according to the number of stitches to be cast on. One way to judge this is to leave 1 inch for each stitch. If you are going to cast on 20 stitches, leave an end 20 inches long. If there is some yarn left over, save it and use it in assembling your knit.

Make a slip knot in the same way shown in the knitted-on method, leaving a long end (1 stitch per inch). Insert the thumb and index finger of your left hand (held to resemble a bird's beak) between the two strands of yarn (fig. 10), then spread these fingers apart (figs. 11 and 12). Insert the tip of the needle under the first strand (fig. 13) and over the third strand (fig. 14), pulling the third strand through the first strand. Tighten and repeat (fig. 15).

Fig. 10. After making slip knot (see figs. 2, 3, and 4), insert left thumb and index finger between two strands of yarn.

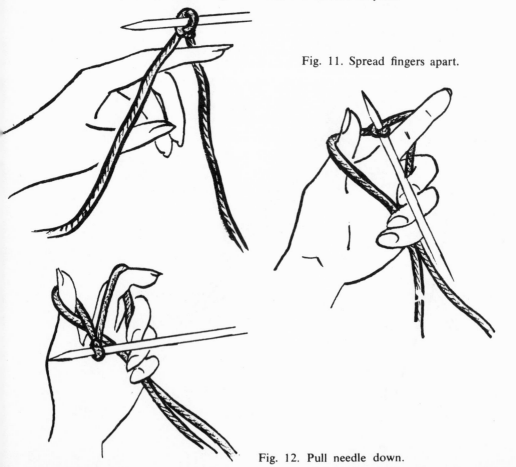

Fig. 11. Spread fingers apart.

Fig. 12. Pull needle down.

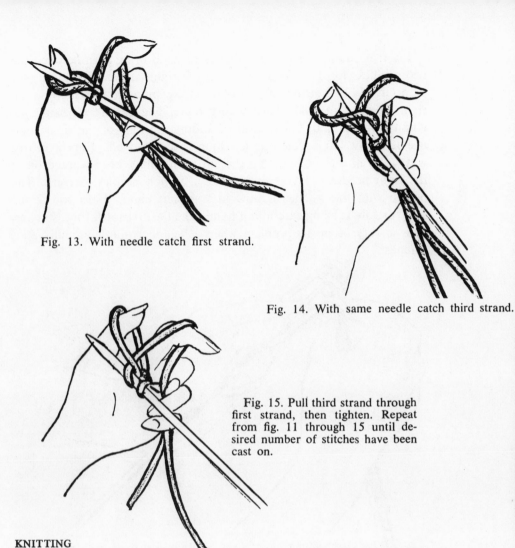

Fig. 13. With needle catch first strand.

Fig. 14. With same needle catch third strand.

Fig. 15. Pull third strand through first strand, then tighten. Repeat from fig. 11 through 15 until desired number of stitches have been cast on.

KNITTING

The European method of knitting with the yarn held in the left hand and the stitches "picked" is not shown in this book because it seems to cause more problems than it solves. You can sometimes obtain more speed, but you'll have some trouble translating certain pattern stitches to the European method. However, it's not impossible. If you already use this method, don't change unless you feel you want to.

Basically, the knitted fabric is made by working over the cast-on stitches one row at a time, from the left-hand needle to the right-hand needle. Each row adds to the length. This is how to do it:

Insert needle in first stitch. With right hand bring yarn between the two needles (fig. 16). With the tip of the right needle force out a new loop (fig. 17). Let the left loop fall off, keeping the new loop on the right needle (fig. 18). This is very much like casting on using the Knitted-on Method, but instead of adding the loop of the right hand needle to the left needle, the left loop is dropped off. Repeat in this way until all the stitches from the left needle have been worked on to the right needle. (1 row completed.) Switch needles, or turn. The needle with the stitches is now in your left hand. Work row 2 the same as row 1, being careful not to mistake the first stitch for 2 stitches. This is very often the problem when a beginner unintentionally adds stitches.

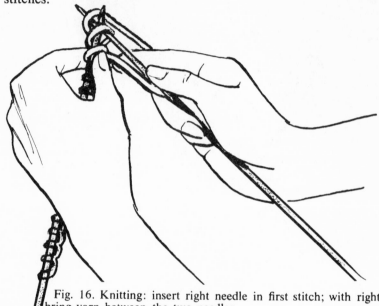

Fig. 16. Knitting: insert right needle in first stitch; with right hand bring yarn between the two needles.

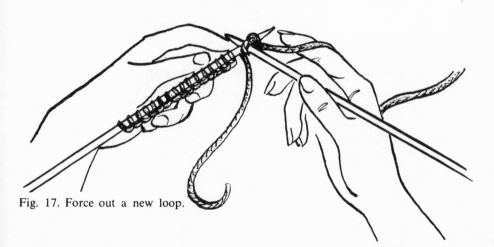

Fig. 17. Force out a new loop.

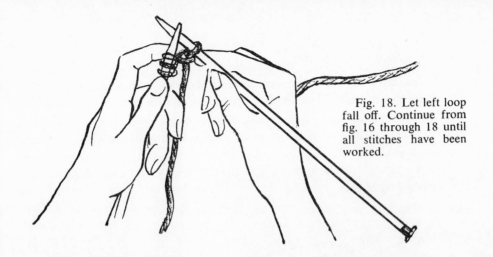

Fig. 18. Let left loop fall off. Continue from fig. 16 through 18 until all stitches have been worked.

PURLING

Purling is really knitting backwards. The yarn is held in front of the work, the needle is inserted into the stitch from the opposite direction, the yarn is hooked over the right needle and the tip of the right needle forces the loop out through the *back* of the stitch (figs. 19 and 20).

Practice the knitting and the purling a little bit, and then go to bind-off method! When you have achieved these basics, you will know enough to begin your samplers.

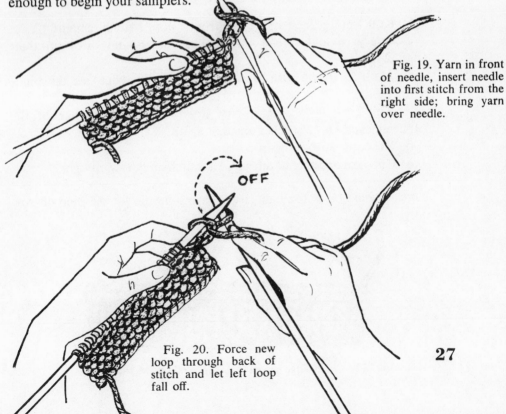

Fig. 19. Yarn in front of needle, insert needle into first stitch from the right side; bring yarn over needle.

OFF

Fig. 20. Force new loop through back of stitch and let left loop fall off.

27

To *bind off* means to decrease stitches in order to form an edge. You can do this most simply by slipping the first of two stitches over the second, and repeating across, as in Method 1 just below.

METHOD 1. This is the bind-off method generally used. It leaves a chain-like edge.

a. Knit 2 stitches, then *slip the 1st knit stitch over the 2nd knit stitch (fig. 21).

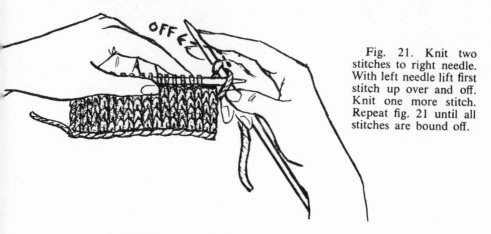

Fig. 21. Knit two stitches to right needle. With left needle lift first stitch up over and off. Knit one more stitch. Repeat fig. 21 until all stitches are bound off.

b. Knit 1 more stitch and repeat from * until 1 stitch remains.

c. Cut yarn and thread through last stitch and draw up tight (fig. 22).

METHOD 2. If you wish to avoid the chain-like edge, use this bind-off method:

a. Knit 2 stitches together, *slip stitch on right needle back to the left needle and knit 2 stitches together again.

b. Repeat from * across row.

c. Cut yarn and thread through last stitch and draw up tight.

Note: If bind-off is too tight, use a larger needle for the bind-off row only.

Fig. 22. Chain edge appearance of bind-off Method 1

METHOD 3. (For the more experienced knitter.) A bind-off method for knit 1, purl 1 ribbing only. This technique is particularly good for raglans worked from the neck down and ending with a ribbed cuff and waistband. Use this method to bind off neckline stitches which are picked up afterwards, too (fig. 23).

a. Thread yarn on a dull pointed needle and insert into the first knit stitch as if to purl, pull yarn through, leaving knit stitch on knitting needle.

b. Insert needle in between knit and purl stitch from the back and insert needle as if to knit (picking up only the front part of the stitch), pull yarn through, leaving stitch on the knitting needle.

c. Insert yarn needle into knit stitch as if to knit and remove stitch. Before working on purl stitch, insert needle into next stitch (skipping purl stitch and in front of work) as if to purl.

d. Insert needle into purl stitch as if to purl and remove stitch. Before working on knit stitch insert needle in between the next 2 stitches from the back and insert needle into purl stitch as if to knit.

Repeat steps c and d until all stitches are bound off.

Fig. 23. Bind-off method 3 for Knit 1, Purl 1 ribbing

2 BASIC STITCHES: KNIT

If you are a beginner, it's a good idea to count your stitches after the first few rows to be sure you are maintaining the same number of stitches you started with. It's very common for a beginner to decrease or increase unwittingly. Don't be afraid to start over again to get it right, even if you have to do it several times. Each time you learn something else.

Abbreviations are added as you read along. If you forget what an abbreviation means, check the Glossary of Terms.

GARTER STITCH—KNITTED (1)

This stitch gives a rough, ridged texture and is achieved by either knitting every row or purling every row. Each ridge is equal to two rows.

Cast on 20 stitches.

Row 1:　Knit across.

Row 2:　Knit across.

Repeat Rows 1 and 2 until piece is square. Bind off.

Fig. 24. Garter stitch

GARTER STITCH—PURLED (2)

This is used primarily to check tension (see below). The general rule for tension is that stitches should be loose enough to slide easily across the needle but not so loose that they fall off.

Cast on 20 stitches.

Row 1: Purl across.

Row 2: Purl across.

Repeat Rows 1 and 2 until piece is square. Bind off.

A sure way to check tension evenness: Make and compare the No. 1 and the No. 2 Garter Stitch samplers. They will look the same, so label them. If the No. 2 Garter Stitch sampler, which was purled, is larger than the No. 1 Knit Garter Stitch sampler, then you are purling looser than you are knitting. Compromise by tightening up on the purling and loosening up on the knitting. It's important to strive for an evenness in tension, which can be checked from time to time by working the first two samplers. We tend to purl more loosely than we knit. Even experienced knitters have improved their work by making this check.

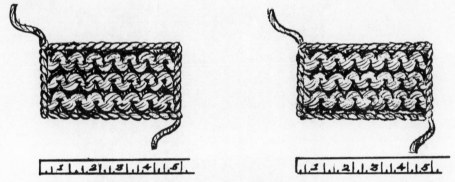

Fig. 25. Measuring knit and purled garter stitch samplers to check for tension evenness.

STOCKINETTE STITCH, KNIT OR PLAIN (3)

This gives a smooth texture and creates a background for a wide variety of trims and finishes. The reverse side can be used in its own right for a different texture. It is natural for the stockinette stitch to curl; press your samplers with a steam iron so they will lie flat. In an

Fig. 26. Stockinette stitch showing reverse side. Either may be used as the right side of a knit.

actual knit the raw edges are either enclosed in side seams or finished with ribbing, a hem, or a crocheted edge, eliminating the curling.

Cast on 20 stitches.

Row 1: Knit across.

Row 2: Purl across.

Repeat Rows 1 and 2 until piece is square. Bind off.

Abbreviations will be used on the next samplers. These abbreviations are standard, and used in knitting instructions everywhere.

st (s)—stitch (es), P—Purl, K—Knit.

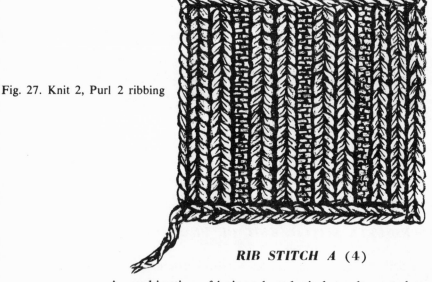

Fig. 27. Knit 2, Purl 2 ribbing

RIB STITCH A (4)

A combination of knit and purl stitches, alternated on the same row and worked so as to produce a ribbed effect. Here is the new technique: Bring the yarn between the needles to the front of the work to purl. Then, to knit, bring the yarn between the needles to the back of the work. It's a particularly good idea to count stitches at the end of the first few rows here, because you can easily forget to change the position of the yarn. Each time you do, a superfluous stitch is added. Cast on 20 sts.

Row 1: *K 2 sts, P 2 sts. Repeat from * across all sts. Repeat this row until piece is square. Bind off loosely in pattern, i.e., knitting the knit stitches and purling the purl stitches. This produces an elastic rib used for waists, wrists, collars or wherever elasticity is needed. Very smart as an overall texture, too.

RIB STITCH B (5)

This stitch is slightly less elastic, and is used in the same way as the first rib.
Cast on 20 sts.
Row 1: *K 1 st, P 1 st. Repeat from * across all sts.
Repeat this row until piece is square. Bind off loosely in pattern (see above).

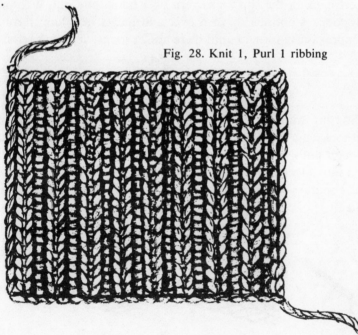

Fig. 28. Knit 1, Purl 1 ribbing

3 BASIC STITCHES: CROCHET

Crochet as used in knitting is most important. Once you learn the following fundamental stitches, you will be able to make whatever crocheted finish or trim you wish, to give your knits that "special" look. Because crochet involves tension, it is learned by "feel," and therefore it takes a lot of practice.

Here, we introduce new abbreviations, as they occur. Chain (ch): The chain is the first step in crochet, just as casting on is the first step in knitting. Try to work it loosely. With your yarn, make a slip knot. Insert hook in the slip knot, yarn over hook, and pull it through as a new loop. Continue to yarn over and pull a new loop through each loop previously formed until there are 21 loops, hereafter referred to as chains.

SINGLE CROCHET (sc) (6)

Starting with the ch 21, turn, insert the hook in the 2nd ch from the hook (fig. 29a) and pull up a loop, yarn over (fig. 29b) and pull through both loops on hook (fig. 29c). (You may take either 1 or 2 strands of chain, but be consistent.) Insert hook in next st of ch and continue to work in this way in each st to end of chain. (20 sc in all.)

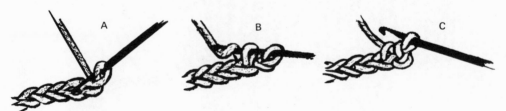

Fig. 29. *A*. Crochet: insert hook into second chain from hook, yarn over; pull through a loop. *B*. Yarn over. *C*. Pull new loop through two loops on hook, repeat *A*, *B*, and *C*, working a single crochet in each chain.

2nd Single Crochet Row: Turn the work, ch 1, *insert hook in top of next st taking up both strands, yarn over and pull up a loop (2 loops on the hook). Yarn over and pull a new loop through both loops on hook. Repeat from * across row. Repeat 2nd row until piece is square. End by cutting yarn and threading the end through the last loop and pulling up tight.

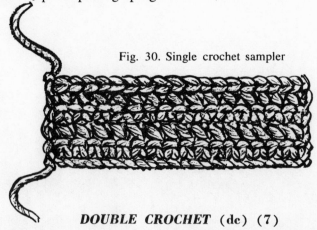

Fig. 30. Single crochet sampler

DOUBLE CROCHET (dc) (7)

Ch 22. Yarn over hook and turn. Insert hook in 3rd ch from hook (fig. 31a), *pull up a loop, yarn over (fig. 31b) and pull a new loop through 2 of the loops (fig. 31c), yarn over again and pull through last 2 loops (fig. 31d). *Yarn over, insert hook in next ch and repeat from * to end of row (20 dc and the ch 2 in all).

2nd Double Crochet Row: Turn the work and ch. 2, *yarn over, insert hook in top of the dc in the row below taking two strands, pull up a loop, yarn over and pull a new loop through 2 of the loops, yarn over again and pull through last 2 loops. Repeat from *. Repeat 2nd row until piece is square. End it.

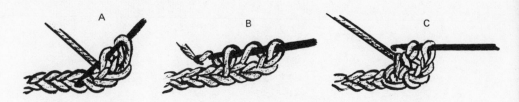

Fig. 31. *A*. Yarn over hook, insert hook into 3rd chain from hook. *B*. Pull up a loop, yarn over. *C*. Pull yarn through two of the loops. *D*. Yarn over again, pull yarn through last two loops.

35

PART II:
TECHNIQUES, TRIMS AND
FINISHINGS

Fig. 32. *A*. Beginning the half double-crochet stitch, *B*. Completed half double-crochet stitch.

HALF DOUBLE CROCHET (hdc) (8)

Ch 22 and turn. Yarn over hook, insert hook in 3rd ch from hook * pull up a loop, yarn over hook (fig. 32a) and pull yarn through all 3 loops (fig. 32b), yarn over hook and insert in next chain, repeat from * across row.

2nd Half Double Crochet Row: Ch 2 and turn. *Yarn over hook, insert hook in top of the hdc below; taking 2 strands, pull up a loop, yarn over and pull yarn through all 3 loops. Repeat Row 2 until piece is square.

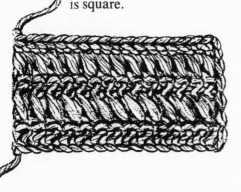

Fig. 33. Half double-crochet sampler

TREBLE CROCHET (tr) (9)

Ch 23 and turn. *Yarn over hook twice, insert hook in the 4th ch from hook (fig. 34a), pull up a loop, yarn over hook and pull yarn through 2 of the loops, yarn over hook and pull yarn through next 2 loops, yarn over hook and through the last 2 loops (fig. 34b), repeat from * across row.

2nd Treble Crochet Row: Ch 3, and turn. 1 tr in each tr of the row below taking 2 strands. Repeat Row 2 until piece is square.

Fig. 34. *A*. Yarn over twice for treble crochet. *B*. Finished treble crochet stitch

4 SHAPING SIDE SEAMS

To shape side seams, you either bind off or decrease, or combine both, as in an armhole shaping. When you bind off (i.e., remove *more than one* stitch at a time), you must do so at the *beginning of a row only:* the beginning of a knit row *and* the beginning of the next purl row, if the bind-off is to be on each side. Decreasing or increasing (*only one* stitch at a time) is done at the beginning and at the end of the *same row,* usually the knit row. Purl rows are generally worked evenly (no decreasing or increasing). The following sampler illustrates the basic shaping technique for knits. Remember, the raw edges are enclosed in side seams.

New Abbreviations: inc (s)—increase (s) psso (pass slipped stitch over knit stitch) dec (s)—decrease (s) tog—together

DECREASE—INCREASE (10)

Cast on 20 sts.

Conventional Decrease Method:

K 2 sts together as if they were 1 st (fig. 35).
Row 1:   K across.
Row 2:   P across.

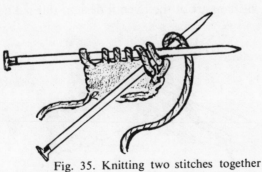

Fig. 35. Knitting two stitches together

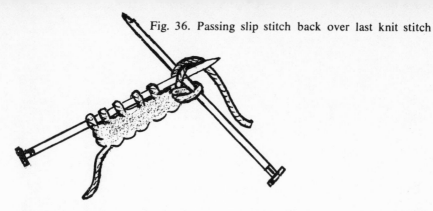

Fig. 36. Passing slip stitch back over last knit stitch

Row 3: K 2 tog, K 16 sts, slip 1 st as to K, K 1, then psso (fig. 36).
Row 4: P across.
Row 5: K 2 tog, K 14, slip 1 st as to K, K 1, then psso.
Row 6: P across.
Row 7: K 2 tog, K 12, slip 1, K 1, psso.
Row 8: P across.
Row 9: K 2 tog, K 10, slip 1, K 1, psso.
Row 10: P across.

Conventional Increase Method:

K 1, do not slip off needle, insert needle in back of the same st just knitted and K again. Now slip this st off needle, 1 st increased (fig. 37).

Row 11: Inc 1, K 10, inc 1.
Row 12: Purl.
Row 13: Inc 1, K 12, inc 1.
Row 14: Purl.
Row 15: Inc 1, K 14, inc 1.
Row 16: Purl.
Row 17: Inc 1, K 16, inc 1.
Row 18: Purl.
Row 19: Inc 1, K 18 sts, inc 1.
Row 20: Purl.

There are times when decreases are worked inside the side seams so as to be a visible part of the overall design; this is known as "fashion"

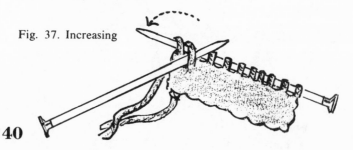

Fig. 37. Increasing

decreasing. Raglan styles are an example of this. The next three samplers illustrate different methods of "fashion" decreasing. See chapter 23 on Raglans, "Back," for more information on how these decreases may be used.

FULL-FASHIONED DECREASE (11)

Cast on 20 sts.
Row 1:   Knit.
Row 2:   Purl.
Row 3:   K 2, K 1, slip back to left needle, slip next st over this st (fig. 38), slip back to right needle, K to within 4 sts of end, slip 1, K 1, psso, K 2.
Row 4:   Purl.
Repeat Rows 3 and 4 until 8 sts remain. Bind off.

DOUBLE DECREASE (12)

More sts are decreased at one time here.
Cast on 40 sts.
Row 1:   Knit.
Row 2:   Purl.
Row 3:   Knit.
Row 4:   Purl.

Fig. 38. Decreasing technique: slipping next stitch back over first stitch

Row 5:   K 2, slip next 2 sts to stitch holder or double-pointed needle. Hold in front of work and * K 1 st from double-pointed needle together with the next st on left hand needle, repeat from * once more (fig. 39). K to within 6 sts of end, slip next 2 sts on double-pointed needle, hold in back of work and * K 1 st from left hand needle together with 1 st from double-pointed needle, repeat from * once more, end K 2.
Repeat Rows 2 through 5 until 24 sts remain. Bind off.

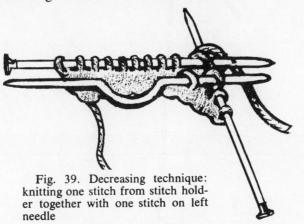

Fig. 39. Decreasing technique: knitting one stitch from stitch holder together with one stitch on left needle

41

TRIPLE DECREASE (13)

This gives the appearance of little tucks in the knitted fabric. The "tucks" look best when worked more than 3 or 4 rows apart. Begin as for the Double Decrease (sampler 12) and work up to Row 5.

Row 5:   K 2, slip 3 sts to stitch holder or double-pointed needle and hold in front of work. K 1 st from double-pointed needle together with the next st on left hand needle 3 times. K to within 8 sts of end, slip next 3 sts on double-pointed needle, hold in back of work. K 1 st from left handle needle together with 1 st from double-pointed needle 3 times, K 2. Repeat Rows 2 through 5.

Note: To achieve a full-fashioned decrease with a look of a cable twist, work the last 2 samplers, reversing the shaping. In other words, hold the stitches on the stitch holder to the back of the work at the beginning of the row, and to the front of the work at the end of the row.

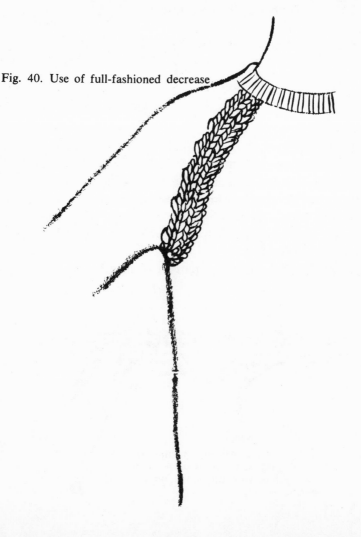

Fig. 40. Use of full-fashioned decrease.

42

5 ASSEMBLING AND FINISHING

The assembling and finishing of a knit can make it either a success or a failure. In working through the following samplers you will not only gain experience because of the practice, but you will become selective as to the kinds of finishes that seem right to you, a further guarantee of your success.

SEAMING TECHNIQUES (14)

Cast on 10 sts. Work stockinette st until strip measures 4 inches. Bind off.
Make 3 strips. Press them with a steam iron on wrong side, through press cloth, for easier handling. Now, the methods of joining them:

Crocheted Slip-Stitch

With right sides of 2 strips together, work a crocheted slip st as follows: Insert crochet hook through the corner of both strips 1 st (2 strands) in. With another piece of yarn underneath work, pull through the first loop. *Insert hook into next st along seam, pull through another loop and pull this loop through the first loop, continue from * (fig. 41). The slip stitch method is particularly good for shoulder seams, setting-in sleeves and attaching collars.

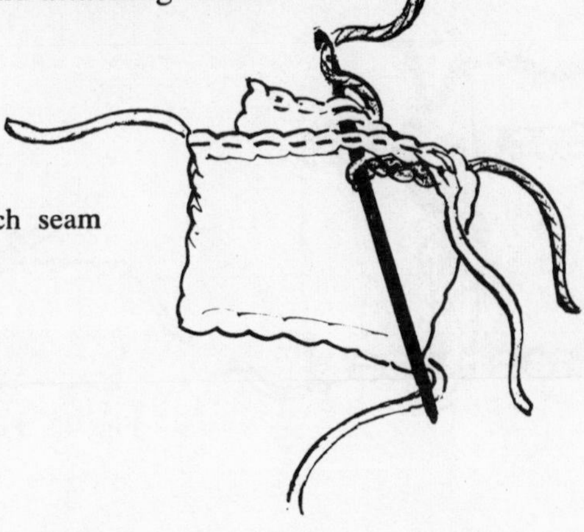

Fig. 41. Working a crocheted slip-stitch seam

Weaving Method

Attach third strip as follows: With right sides facing and a yarn needle, insert needle in lower left corner 1 stitch in, from back to front, leaving a 1-inch to 2-inch end at the back. Insert needle catching 2 horizontal or cross threads one stitch in on right side, then 2 threads one stitch in on left side. Work from side to side in this manner. If the knitting is very even, this method can be used in the center of the last stitch instead of one stitch in (fig. 42).

The weaving method may be used for all side seams on skirts and tops, and in assembling raglans.

Assembling the Knit

To assemble a knit, seam shoulders first, then set in the sleeves, using the slip-stitch method. Then, using the weaving method, sew the side and sleeve seams. Neckline and border stitches are picked up after assembling.

Picking Up Stitches

If a cardigan, pick up stitches with a straight knitting needle; if a pullover, use a circular needle or double-pointed needles. Always work with the right side facing.

*With knitting needle and yarn insert needle 1 stitch deep (2 strands), wrap yarn around needle and pull through a loop. Repeat from * (fig. 43).

KITCHENER OR WEAVING STITCH (15)

This method is used for closing the toes of socks, for shoulder

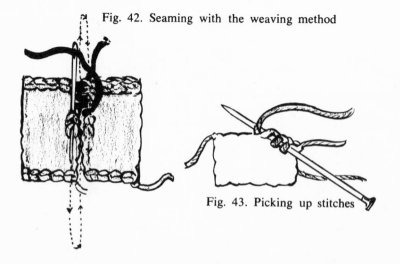

Fig. 42. Seaming with the weaving method

Fig. 43. Picking up stitches

seams, for adding length or welding two pieces together without producing a noticeable seam.

Cast on 20 sts.

Work in stockinette st until piece measures 2½ inches, ending with a P row. Leave on needle. Make two.

Hold needles parallel with wrong sides of work together. Thread end of a contrasting color yarn needle and weave sts together as follows: (The contrasting color helps you see the stitches more clearly. The same color yarn would be used, of course, in the actual use of this technique.)

1. Insert needle through first st of front needle as if to P and leave it on.
2. * Insert needle through first st of back needle as if to K and leave it on.
3. Insert needle through first st of front needle as if to K and take it off.
4. Insert needle through next st of front needle as if to P and leave it on.
5. Insert needle through first st of back needle as if to P and take it off. Repeat from * until all sts are joined.

If you work better from a diagram than from written instructions, the following diagram (fig. 44) is for you. This gives you two ways to learn a difficult technique.

Start with Step 1, continue through Step 11, Repeat from Step 4 through Step 11 until all sts are worked.

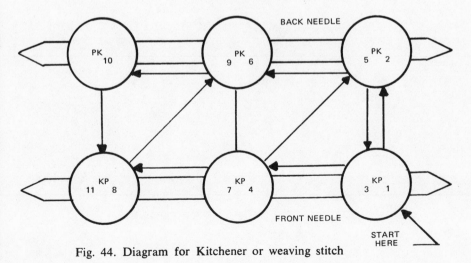

EACH CIRCLE REPRESENTS ONE STITCH

Fig. 44. Diagram for Kitchener or weaving stitch

CLOSING A SEAM WHILE BINDING OFF (16)

Another method, and a simpler one, for closing the toes of socks and assembling shoulder seams is to hold the needles parallel with the purl sides out and insert a third knitting needle as if to purl, into the first st of the back needle and into the first st of the front needle, and then purl together. Do the same thing in the next 2 sts. Two sts on right needle. Now lift the first st over and off the 2nd st, binding off. Continue purling the sts from the back and front needle together and binding off at the same time until all sts have been worked off.

6 HEMS

Adapting to knitting some of the finishing techniques used in sewing has brought us various hems, hemlines and facings which expand the fashion possibilities of hand knits. The following techniques show how these may be done.

CONVENTIONAL HEMS (17)

Cast on 20 sts.
Work stockinette st for 1 inch ending with a P row.
HEMLINE 1. P next 2 rows. (This gives you one row of purl on the right side which becomes the hemline.) The purled row allows the turned-under part of the hem to lie flat. Continue stockinette st for 2 more inches. Bind off. Sew hem with yarn and a whip stitch.

Whip Stitch

To hem, turn under the bottom of the knit, which will become the underside of your hem. With your threaded yarn needle, catch one strand from the edge of knit and one strand from the body, draw together, and repeat every quarter of an inch.
HEMLINE 2. On hemline row only (work sampler same as above) K in back of the stitch, thus twisting each stitch. This tightens up the hemline row which is another way to help the turned-under part of the hem to lie flat.
HEMLINE 3. On hemline row only (work sampler same as above) K with a needle 1 or 2 sizes larger, giving a stretched stitch row for a smooth hemline. This achieves the same effect as the first 2 hems but without a noticeable hemline.

REFINED HEM (18)

Cast on 20 sts with finer needles.

With needles 1 or 2 sizes smaller than the rest of the sampler, work stockinette st until hemline. Change to larger needles and continue stockinette st for 2 more inches. Bind off. In this way the underside of the hem is a finer stitch and the hem becomes less bulky. The top side of the hem may also be done on the finer needles, using the larger needles for the turning row only.

HEMS USING HEAVY YARN. If the yarn has plies which can be separated, work the underside of the hem with fewer plies, cutting away the unneeded plies as you go, or use a finer yarn for the underside of the hem.

PICOT HEM (19)

This picot hemline is so pretty that it requires no other trim. Work the same technique at the neckline and sleeves (See hem on fig. 46).

Cast on 20 sts.

Work stockinette st for 1 inch ending with a P row.

Hemline Row: K 1, *YO (yarn over) making an extra stitch, K 2 tog (fig. 45); repeat from * across row, end with a K 1. Resume stockinette st for 2 more inches. Bind off. An alternate way to do this is to K 2 or 3 sts before each YO, K 2 tog.

Note: Hems may be joined by knitting or purling 1 st from the needle together with one st from the bottom of the hem (cast-on edge) and continuing across the row, instead of using a whip stitch after it is complete. Knit the stitches together if it is a knit row and purl the stitches together if it is a purl row (fig. 46).

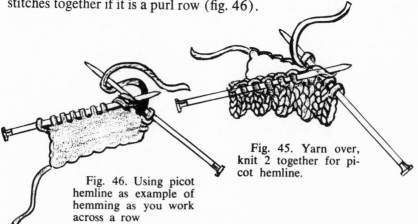

Fig. 45. Yarn over, knit 2 together for picot hemline.

Fig. 46. Using picot hemline as example of hemming as you work across a row

FACINGS (20)

Cast on 11 sts.

METHOD 1.

Row 1: K 5, slip 1 as to P, K 5.
Row 2: P.
The slipped 6th st on every K row becomes the folding line for the facing. Repeat Rows 1 and 2 for desired length. 3 inches for sampler.

METHOD 2.

Twist the 6th st when working it on the K rows and the P rows.
These methods help the turned-under part to lie flat much like the hemlines.

MITERED CORNER, USING A HEM AND A FACING (21)

Using both hem and facing is the ultimate in refinement. This is a technique you would use for necklines as well as for the bottom of a jacket or coat.
Cast on 15 sts.

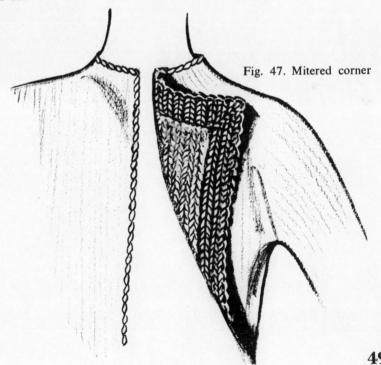

Fig. 47. Mitered corner

49

Row 1:   Inc in the first st as to P (using the knitting-on method just cast on 1 stitch inserting needle as to P). P across row.

Row 2:   K next row, inc in last st. Repeat these 2 rows twice more (6 rows in all).

Row 7:   Inc in first st as to K, K across row. This row forms hemline.

Row 8:   K across row and inc in last st.

Row 9:   P next row, inc in first st.

Row 10: K to 3 sts, from end, sl the third st from end as to P, K 1, inc in end st.

Row 11: Inc as to P in first st and P across row.

Row 12: K to last 5 sts, sl the fifth st as to P, K 3, inc in end st (27 sts are on the needle). Continue purling the P rows and knitting the K rows, slipping the same st as to P on the K rows, for 2½ more inches. Bind off. Sew hem and facing with a whip stitch.

7 PUTTING IN A ZIPPER

Placing a zipper properly in a knit is sometimes difficult. It is the preparation rather than the actual sewing-in of the zipper that serves to solve this problem.

PREPARATION (22)

The following suggestions will be helpful. Make samplers, leaving a split for the zipper, and try the different methods. The basic sampler instructions are:

Cast on 20 sts.

Work stockinette st for 1 inch. Select which method you want to try (see below) and incorporate it into these instructions.

Row 1:   K10. With another piece of yarn K the last 10 sts.

Row 2:   P.

Repeat these 2 rows, taking up the other piece of yarn to work the 10 sts at the end of the rows. (This maintains the split.) When piece measures length of zipper to be used, bind off.

When leaving an opening for a zipper in the knitted fabric, you may (1) increase 1 st each side of the opening and slip this st every other row for a selvedge edge, or (2) make these increased stitches in a garter stitch, to be turned under before you sew in the zipper. (3) If you plan to work a row of simple crochet before sewing in the zipper, you may also *decrease* 1 st on each side of the beginning of the opening. This decrease compensates for the extra stitch added by the crochet, and makes a neater finish. Experiment and decide which kind of opening you like best, taking into account the weight and texture of yarn used.

INSERTION

1. Baste zipper opening from the right side with sewing thread.
2. Attach zipper from the inside, pinning or basting it first, then work small running back sts, with sewing thread so that sts do not show from the right side.
3. Remove basting, and steam slightly.

8 BUTTONHOLES

Neat buttonholes in hand knitting are one of the marks of a professional. All too often, they're a job that the knitter leaves to the knit shop. With a little practice, a beginner can do just as well as a professional. The following buttonholes begin with a simple method that gets more refined as you read along. Try them all. A word about the buttonhole placement. With each buttonhole, with the exception of the cut-in (sampler 25), you must decide on the placement *before* you work the right front of your cardigan. Use the left front as a guide. Mark the top and the bottom for placement, and wherever necessary in between, at even intervals.

CONVENTIONAL KNIT-IN BUTTONHOLE (23)

Cast on 12 sts.
Work stockinette st for 1 inch ending with a P row.
Buttonhole Row 1: K 4, bind off 4 (6 sts are worked, then the 5th st is lifted over the 6th st to start the bind off, K 4).
Row 2: P 4, cast on 4, using the knitting-on method, P 4, (turn work for the cast-on sts, turn back again and finish row).
Continue stockinette st working 2 more buttonholes at 1-inch intervals.
Bind off.

REFINED KNIT-IN BUTTONHOLE (24)

This is an improvement over the conventional buttonhole; it is neater.
Cast on 12 sts.
Work stockinette st for 1 inch, ending with a P row.

53

Buttonhole Row 1: K 4, slip next 2 sts to right hand needle as to P, *skip st on left hand needle, slip next st or 2nd st over first st and drop it off, sl 1st st on right hand needle to left hand needle and repeat from * until 3 sts remain. Sl remaining st to right hand needle (4 sts in all on right-hand needle), turn, cast on 4 sts using the knit-on method, turn, with right needle pick up st in the row below before sts on left hand needle (fig. 48), place on left hand needle, K 5.

Row 2: P 4, P lifted st together with first cast on st, P 7. Continue stockinette st working 2 more buttonholes at 1-inch intervals. Bind off.

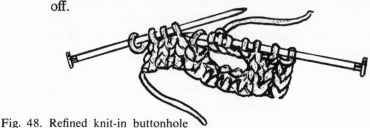

Fig. 48. Refined knit-in buttonhole

CUT-IN BUTTONHOLE (25)

The size and placement of buttons, and therefore of buttonholes, can often better be determined after a knit has been finished. Therefore, the great advantage of this cut-in buttonhole is that it's worked after everything else is done. It takes practice, and making a cut into the material is scary at first, but it's well worth the effort.

Cast on 12 sts.

Work stockinette st for 4 inches. Bind off.

Work cut-in buttonholes as follows: Pull out horizontal thread in center of where buttonhole is to be placed, slit it, free 3 loops on the top and 3 loops on the bottom (fig. 49). With a crochet hook and another piece of yarn work a slip st in the lower right corner, in each of the three bottom loops in the lower left corner, and in the upper left corner, in the 3 top loops and the upper right corner, and join into

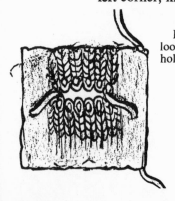

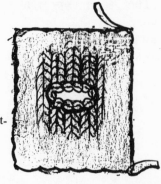

Fig. 49. Freeing loops for cut-in buttonhole

Fig. 50. Finished cut-in buttonhole

the lower right corner again. Slip st may be worked with K or P side facing or a sc may be substituted. Leave the ends at least an inch long and weave them in and out of the back of the work (fig. 50).

The buttonholes may be made larger or smaller by freeing more or less loops.

BUTTONHOLE USING CONTRASTING COLOR YARN (26)

If you like the appearance of the cut-in buttonhole but don't like cutting into the fabric, this is the buttonhole for you. Another advantage is that the yarn, rather than being cut, is left in a loop to finish the buttonhole, thus leaving fewer loose ends which must then be worked in. *Remember that buttonhole placement must be predetermined.*

Cast on 12 sts, with main color.

Work stockinette st for 1 inch ending with a P row.

Buttonhole Row 1: K 4, drop main color, take up a 3-inch strand of contrasting color, and K the next 4 sts, drop contrasting color and take up main color leaving about a 14-inch strand, looped in the back, K remaining 4 sts (fig. 51). Continue stockinette st using main color and repeat buttonhole row at 1 inch intervals twice more. Bind off.

Finishing Buttonhole: Cut through center of long strand of main color, remove the contrasting color and, from wrong side, work a slip st through loops, fasten off this side, then work other side and fasten off. Weave in ends.

YARN-OVER BUTTONHOLE (27)

Another useful and simple buttonhole method is to make a small button opening by working a yarn over, K 2 together, opposite where buttons are to be placed.

Fig. 51. Buttonhole sampler using contrasting color yarn

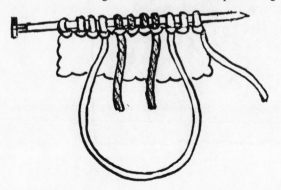

55

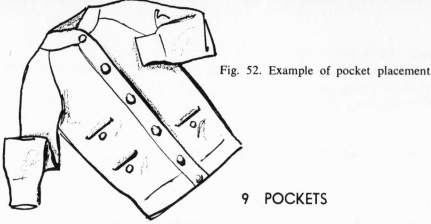

Fig. 52. Example of pocket placement

9 POCKETS

Pockets, in addition to their usefulness, offer another aspect of knitted fashion design. Variations in pocket placement and your selection of a pocket trim may add just the accent you need to enhance one of your own original designs.

FOLDED POCKET (28)

This makes a very neat plain pocket. No other finish or trim is necessary.

Cast on 20 sts.

Work stockinette st for 4 inches, ending with a P row; K 5 sts, then sl these sts to a stitch holder. K the next 10 sts, then sl the last 5 sts to another stitch holder.

Work in stockinette st on the 10 sts until piece measures 7 ins, ending with a P row.

Attaching the Pocket

K the 10 sts, fold pocket and slip the 5 sts on holder to left needle and K them.

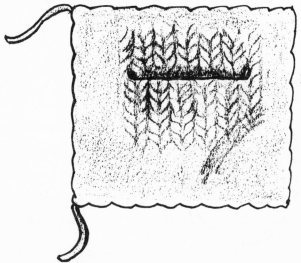

Fig. 53. Folded pocket

Next Row—P across, slipping remaining 5 sts on holder to left needle and P them.
Continue stockinette st for 1 inch. Bind off.
Whip or sl stitch sides of pocket together.

INSERTED POCKET (29)

This pocket leaves an edge which allows a crocheted or knitted trim to be used.
Pocket Lining—Cast on 12 sts. Work stockinette st for 2 inches. Place on a stitch holder.
Pocket—Cast on 20 sts. Work stockinette st for 2½ inches, ending with a P row. K 4, bind off 12, K 4. Insert lining as follows: P 4, slip lining stitches (wrong side facing) on left needle and P these, then P remaining 4. Continue stockinette st for 1 more inch. Bind off. Sew lining to pocket with a yarn needle and a whip stitch.

PATCH POCKET (30)

This pocket can be trimmed also, if desired.
Lining—Cast on 20 sts. Work stockinette st for 4 inches. Bind off. (This represents the body of the knit to which a patch pocket can be attached.)
Patch—Cast on 12 sts. Work stockinette st for 2½ inches. Bind off. Sew to lining, using duplicate st on bottom and weaving st on sides (fig. 54). (See chap. 5, "Weaving Method.")

For a Flap Pocket

Work reverse stockinette st; dec 1 st for each side every K row 3 times, or work straight for desired length, or shape in whatever way desired. Bind off. Add a button for a trim variation.

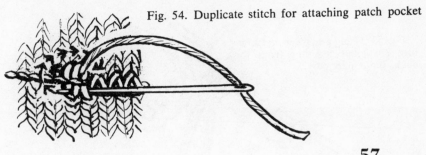

Fig. 54. Duplicate stitch for attaching patch pocket

10 SHAPING WITH DARTS

The knitted fabric itself tends to take on the shape of the figure wearing it, but additional shaping of knits, using darts, adds a refinement you will want to include in all your work. The bustline shaping is particularly becoming and adds much to the finished look.

SKIRT DART (31)

This dart sampler, used for skirts or the skirt part of dresses, uses matched decreases. Darts used in skirts add a refinement in shaping because not all of the stitches to be decreased from the hip to the waist have to come off on the sides.

Cast on 40 sts.

Row 1:   Knit.

Row 2:   Purl.

Row 3:   Knit.

Row 4:   Purl.

Row 5:   K 10, place a marker or tie contrasting color yarn around the needle, K 20, place a marker, K 10.

Row 6:   P.

Row 7:   K to within 2 sts of the marker, slip these 2 sts one at a time to right needle as to K. Place back on left needle without removing right needle, and K these 2 sts tog from the back (fig. 55),

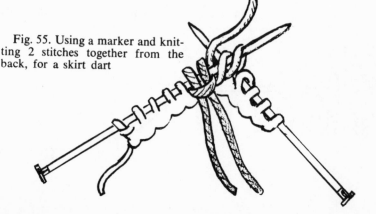

Fig. 55. Using a marker and knitting 2 stitches together from the back, for a skirt dart

pass marker, K next 2 sts together. Repeat before and after next marker every 4th row until 20 sts remain. Bind off.

DRESS DART WITH A LIFTED INCREASE (32)

This makes a beautiful dart for a one-piece dress. It gives a very smooth appearance. Use it to shape the sides in a dress worked on a circular needle, too.

Cast on 21 sts.

(For lifted increase pick up loop of stitch below)

Row 1: Knit.
Row 2: Purl.
Row 3: K 8 sts, K 2 tog, K 1, K 2 tog, K 8.
Row 4: Purl.
Row 5: Knit.
Row 6: Purl.
Row 7: K 7 sts, K 2 tog, K 1, K 2 tog, K 7.
Repeat Rows 4, 5, and 6.
Row 11: K 6 sts, K 2 tog, K 1, K 2 tog, K 6.
Repeat Rows 4, 5, and 6.
Row 15: K 6, inc 1 using the lifted increase technique (see fig. 56), K 1, inc 1, K 6.
Repeat Rows 4, 5, and 6.
Row 19: K 7, inc 1, K 1, inc 1, K 7.
Repeat Rows 4, 5, and 6.
Row 23: K 8, inc 1, K 1, inc 1, K 8.
Repeat Rows 4, 5, and 6.
Bind off.

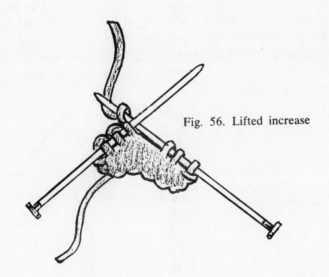

Fig. 56. Lifted increase

Variation

A dress dart may be made by K 2 together once at each dart point to the waist and increasing one stitch at each dart point to the bust, instead of decreasing and increasing 2 at a time as above.

BUSTLINE DARTS

These darts allow you to have more inches over the bust where fullness is required without adding more inches to the sides. Knits take on a more feminine shape using these techniques.

Split Dart (33)

If you want shaping, but with a tailored look, this dart is for you.
Cast on 40 sts.
Work in stockinette st for 1 inch, ending with a P row.
At the beginning of the next 6 rows (K and P rows) bind off 5 sts, making 3 slopes on each side. At the beginning of the next 2 rows cast on 15 sts, using the knitted-on method. (See "Casting-on", chap. l.)
Continue stockinette st for 1 more inch.
Bind off.
Sew together with a crocheted slip stitch or the duplicate stitch.

Dart Using Short-Row Knitting Technique (34)

This bustline dart adds a beautiful and subtle shaping which you will want to use in every shell, cardigan, dress or coat you make.
Cast on 40 sts.
Work in stockinette st for 1 inch, ending with a P row.
Row 1: K 35 sts, turn work (5 remaining sts not worked).
Row 2: *Yarn to back of work, sl first st from *right hand* needle to left hand needle, *yarn to front* of work, sl the sl st from left hand needle back to right hand needle, * (this produces a hole, which will be eliminated when working across the completed short rows); P 30, turn work.

Fig. 57. Split bustline dart

60

Row 3: *Yarn to front of work, sl first st on *right hand* needle to left hand needle, *yarn to back,* sl the sl st back to right hand needle, *K25, turn work.

Row 4: Repeat between *'s of Row 2, P 20, turn work.

Row 5: Repeat between *'s of Row 3, K 15, turn work.

Row 6: Repeat between *'s of Row 2, P 10, turn work.

Row 7: Repeat between *'s of Row 3, K 10, *insert needle in front of loop wrapped around stitch as well as the next st and knit together* (fig. 58). K 4, repeat between *'s, K 4, repeat between *'s, end K 4. This completes the left side of the dart.

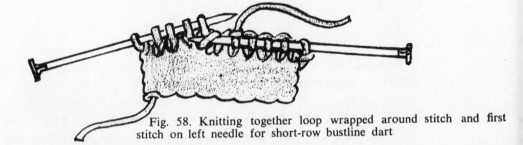

Fig. 58. Knitting together loop wrapped around stitch and first stitch on left needle for short-row bustline dart

Row 8: P 25 *insert needle in back of loop wrapped around next st and in next st as well and P tog* (fig. 59). P 4, repeat between *'s, P 4, repeat between *'s end P 4. This completes right side of the dart.

Note: You may bind off shoulders using the short row technique: bind off after Row 8 has been completed.

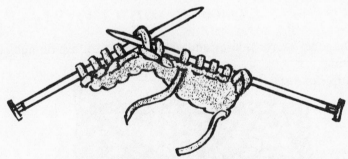

Fig. 59. Purling together loop wrapped around stitch and first stitch on left needle for short-row bustline dart

61

11 PATTERN STITCHES: SIMPLE TEXTURE

One of the most delightful aspects of knitting is that you make your own fabric. The variety is limitless.

SEED STITCH (35)

This pebbled stitch adds a richness to the knitted fabric you will like, either as an overall texture or for trim.

Cast on 21 sts.

Row 1: *K 1 st, P 1 st. Repeat from * across all sts. The last st will be a K st. Repeat this row until piece is square. Bind off.

Fig. 60. Seed stitch

DIAGONAL STITCH (36)

Diagonal weave fabrics add great interest to fashion and so it is in knitting.

Multiple of 8 sts.

Fig. 61. Diagonal stitch

62

Cast on 24 sts.

Row 1:   *K 4, P 4, repeat from * across row.
Row 2:   P 1, *K 4, P 4, repeat from * across row, end P 3.
Row 3:   K 2, *P 4, K 4, repeat from * across row, end K 2.
Row 4:   P 3, *K 4, P 4, repeat from * across row, end P 1.
Row 5:   *P 4, K 4, repeat from * across row.
Row 6:   K 1, *P 4, K 4, repeat from * across row, end K 3.
Row 7:   P 2, *K 4, P 4, repeat from * across row, end P 2.
Row 8:   K 3, *P 4, K 4, repeat from * across row, end K 1.
Repeat Rows 1 through 8 for pattern.

TWIST STITCH (37)

This is a plain stitch with an occasional twist for interest.
Cast on 19 sts.
Row 1:   Knit.
Row 2:   Purl.
Row 3:   K 3, sl as to K, across.
Row 4:   P 3,*. slip 1 st. P next st, pick up sl st, and P it, P 2, repeat
from across row.
Repeat these 4 rows for pattern.

Fig. 62. Twist stitch

CABLE STITCHES

The next two pattern stitches (Standard and Mock Cable) are
particularly effective on sweaters. On a pullover, they can be used to
ornament the front; on a cardigan, they look especially well as borders.

You may wish to use them, as shown in figure 63, running along the center of a sleeve, or in lieu of ribbing.

Standard Cable Stitch (38)

A large bold stitch which resembles the twists of a rope and most appropriate for sportswear. It can be worked into the fabric or you just cast on enough sts to make the cable twist and sew on for a trim. Cast on 20 sts.

Row 1:   K 5, P 1, K 8, P 1, K 5.
Row 2:   P 5, K 1, P 8, K 1, P 5.
Row 3:   K 5, P 1, K 8, P 1, K 5.
Row 4:   P 5, K 1, P 8, K 1, P 5.
Row 5:   K 5, P 1, place next 4 sts on a cable holder and hold in back of work, K next 4 sts, then K the 4 sts off the cable holder, P 1, K 5.
Row 6:   P 5, K 1, P 8, K 1, P 5.
Row 7:   K 5, P 1, K 8, P 1, K 5.
Row 8:   P 5, K 1, P 8, K 1, P 5.
Row 9:   K 5, P 1, K 8, P 1, K 5.
Row 10:   P 5, K 1, P 8, K 1, P 5.
Row 11:   K 5, P 1, K 8, P 1, K 5.
Row 12:   P 5, K 1, P 8, K 1, P 5.
Row 13:   Repeat Row 5.

Work 1 more cable twist and bind off.

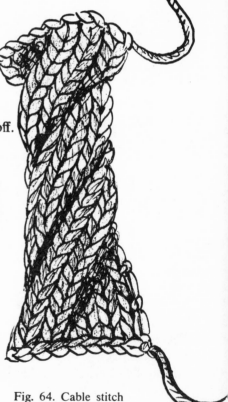

Fig. 64. Cable stitch

Fig. 63. Use of cable stitch trim

Mock Cable (**39**)

A more delicate cable.

Cast on 21 sts.

Row 1:   K 5, P 1, K 4, P 1, K 4, P 1, K 5.

Row 2:   P 5, K 1, P 4, K 1, P 4, K 1, P 5.

Row 3:   K 5, P 1, K 4th st over and leave on needle (fig. 66), then K first, second, and third sts and sl 4th st off P 1, sl next st on cable holder and hold in front of work, K next 3 sts, then K first st off cable hook, P 1, K 5.

Row 4:   P 5, K 1, P 4, K 1, P 4, K 1, P 5.

Row 5:   K 5, P 1, K 4, P 1, K 4, P 1, K 5.

Row 6:   P 5, K 1, P 4, K 1, P 4, K 1, P 5.

Row 7:   Same as Row 3.

Repeat last 4 rows until piece measures 4 inches.

Bind off.

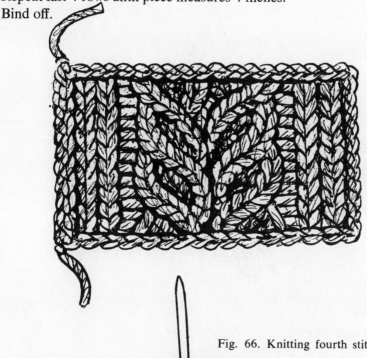

Fig. 65. Mock cable

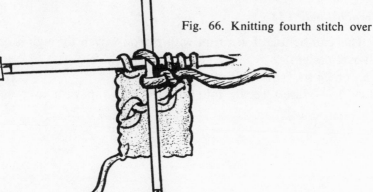

Fig. 66. Knitting fourth stitch over

Lacy Cable (40)

A lacy feminine stitch with the cable touch. A beautiful allover pattern as well as an insert. This uses the YO (or yarn over) technique, which is what gives the lacy appearance.

Cast on 20 sts.

Row 1: *Purl 2, YO (keep yarn in front), sl 1 as if to K, K 1, psso, K 2 tog, YO (bring yarn to front, over needle and back to the front to get ready for the P), repeat from * across row ending with P 2.

Row 2: *K 2, P 4, repeat from * across row ending with K 2.

Row 3: *P 2, K 4, repeat from * across row ending with P 2.

Row 4: Same as Row 2.

Repeat these 4 rows until piece is square. Bind off.

Fig. 67. Use of a pattern stitch insert

French Cable (41)

This can be used for a trim with ribbon woven through it or as an all-over design.

Cast on 24 sts. (Multiple of 6 sts)

Row 1: *Insert needle into st as to K, wrap yarn over needle 3

66

times. Finish knitting sts, repeat from * across row.

Row 2:   *Slip 6 large loops as to P, lift sts 1, 2, and 3 over sts 4, 5, and 6. P each st.

Repeat from * across row.

Row 3:   Knit.

Row 4:   Purl.

Fig. 68. Use of a French cable insert

Fig. 69. French cable with ribbon detail

POPCORN STITCHES

The following three stitches make beautiful all-over patterns, or may be used on just sleeves or fronts, together with the plain stockinette stitch. Work them in clusters, or in horizontal, vertical or diagonal stripes.

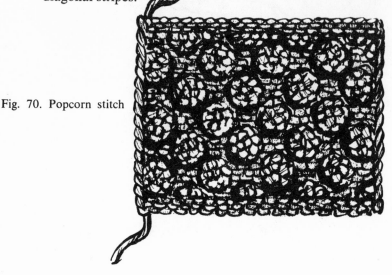

Fig. 70. Popcorn stitch

Popcorn Stitch (42)

A bold, knotty, deeply textured stitch—very rich-looking. Increase 5 sts in one st working back and forth on the 5 sts and decreasing back down to 1 st again.

Cast on 20 sts.

Row 1:   Purl.

Row 2:   * K 4, ** K 1, P 1, K 1, P 1, K 1, ** all in next st. Be sure to bring yarn to the front for purl and to the back for knit. Turn, K 5 sts of popcorn, turn, P 5, then with left needle slip 2nd, 3rd, 4th and 5th st on right needle over first st. Repeat from * across row, ending with a K 5.

Work 4 rows of stockinette st. and repeat Row 2. Continue until 4 rows of popcorns have been completed. Bind off.

Cast on 20 sts.

Row 1: Purl.

Row 2: *K 4, K 7 sts *loosely* into next st alternating from front to back for bubble (repeating the conventional increase), repeat from * across ending with a K 5.

Row 3: P 5, P 7 sts of bubble tog, * P 4, P 7 sts of bubble tog, repeat from * end with a P 4.

Work 4 rows of stockinette st and repeat Row 2, and Row 3. Continue until 4 rows of bubbles have been completed. Work 2 rows of stockinette st and bind off.

Small Popcorn Stitch (43)

This is a more delicate, but deeply textured stitch. Only 3 sts increased in 1 here.

Cast on 19 sts.

Row 1: Purl.

Row 2: K 1, * in the next st, K 1, P 1, K 1 (3 sts made from 1 st) P 3 tog, repeat from * ending in the next st, K 1, P 1, K 1 (3 sts made) K 1.

Row 3: Purl.

Row 4: K 1, * 3 tog, in the next st, K 1, P 1, K 1 (3 sts made) repeat from * ending P 3 tog, K 1.

Repeat these 4 rows until piece is square. Bind off.

Note: There will always be 2 extra sts when Row 2 has been completed.

Bubble Stitch (44)

Resembles puffs of yarn scattered on a plain background. Yarn with a furry, fuzzy fiber in it lends itself to this stitch very well. Seven stitches are increased in one stitch here.

12 ADVANCED TEXTURE STITCHES

Understanding Multiples

What does it mean when pattern-stitch instructions include as part of the information a multiple of stitches? Using the next pattern stitch as an example, sampler 45 (multiple of 4 plus 3) tells us that the number of stitches to be cast on must be a number divisible by 4, or multipliable by 4, plus 3 extra stitches. $4 \times 4 = 16$ plus 3 or 19 stitches; $4 \times 5 = 20$ plus 3 or 23 stitches. This maintains the pattern as each row is added on. Without this information, the pattern stitch could be thrown off.

The advanced texture stitches were selected to represent the different techniques used in fancy knitting so that you would be able to read and understand any stitch instructions. If you can do the following stitches, you can do almost anything.

EASY CLUSTER PATTERN (45)

Multiple of 4 plus 3.

This is a particularly pretty stitch.

Cast on 19 sts.

Row 1: (Right side) Knit.

Row 2: P 1, *K 1, P 3 tog, and *leave on needle* YO, p the same 3 sts tog again and take off needle (cluster st)* end K 1, P 1.

Row 3: Knit.

Row 4: *Work a cluster by purling first 3 sts tog, etc., K 1, *work a cluster on last 3 sts also.

Repeat these 4 rows until piece is square. Bind off.

Fig. 71. Easy cluster stitch

BASKET-WEAVE STITCH (46)

An unusual stitch that looks woven and has a firmness that makes it very good for coats, skirts and suits.

Cast on 20 sts. If using 2-needle method of casting on, P first row.

Row 1: *Insert right-hand needle from back of work to front between first and second sts on left hand needle. Bring front loop of second st to back of work, K this loop; then K the first st of front loop of st, slip both sts off left hand needle. Repeat from * across row.

Row 2: P 1, *P the second st on left hand needle and leave on needle, P the first st, on left hand needle, slip both sts off needle, repeat from * end P 1.

Repeat these 2 rows for pattern.

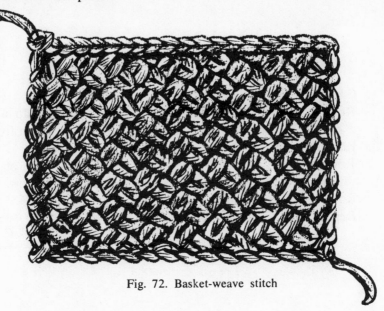

Fig. 72. Basket-weave stitch

This stitch has a dimensional quality that is most becoming and that changes with the size of the needle. Try this stitch using large needles (10½, 11 or 13) and using two strands of yarn in monochromatic colors (two shades of pink, or beige, or blue and green tog). Knitting in the row below is a new technique here.

Cast on an even number of sts—Cast on 20 sts for sampler.

Row 1: K 1, K in the row below (fig. 73); repeat to end of row.

Row 2: Knit.

Row 3: K in the row below, K 1, repeat to end of row.

Row 4: Knit.

Repeat these 4 rows for pattern.

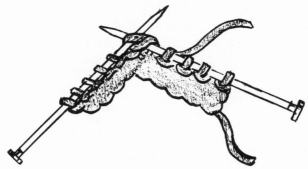

Fig. 73. Knitting in the row below in waffle stitch

ZIGZAG PATTERN (48)

This gives an interesting texture with a zigzag look.

Cast on 19 sts—Multiple of 3 plus 1.

Row 1: P 1, *K 2nd st on left hand needle but do not slip off needle, K first st and slip both sts off needle, P 1, repeat from *.

Row 2: K 1, * P 2, K 1, repeat from * across row.

Row 3: P 1, *K into back of 2nd st but do not slip off needle, K first st and slip both sts off, P 1, repeat from * across row.

Row 4: Repeat Row 2.

Repeat these 4 rows for pattern.

OPEN-WORK STITCH (49)

Cast on 20 sts.

Beginning on right side, work garter stitch for uneven number of rows.

Row 1: (Wrong side) *Insert needle into stitch as to K, YO needle twice, and knit pulling both YO loops through, repeat from *.

Row 2: *(Sl 1 as to P, drop yarn overs off left hand needle) 4

Fig. 74. Using open-work stitch as an insert

times. Pull sts down forming long sts, sl the 4 long sts back to left hand needle. Counting the 4 sts as 1, K, P, K, P into this st. Slip worked st off. Repeat from *.

Repeat these 2 rows for pattern, with garter stitch worked in between.

LEAF STITCH (50)

This is a lacy kind of stitch that is feminine and elegant, and would be beautiful worked into any fashion. It's a challenge to a beginning knitter, but once the pattern is established it becomes easier.

Cast on 25 sts—Multiple of 8 sts plus 1. Slip all sl sts as to K.

Row 1: K 3 *YO, sl 1 as to K, K 2 tog, psso, YO, K 5 repeat from * across, ending YO, sl 1 K 2 tog, psso, YO, K 3.

Row 2: And all even rows following—Purl.

73

Row 3: K 2 tog, K 1, *YO, K 3, YO, K 1, sl 1, K 2 tog, psso, K 1, repeat from * across ending YO, K 3, YO, K 1, K 2 tog.

Row 4: Purl.

Row 5: K 2 tog, *YO, K 5, YO, sl 1, K 2 tog, psso, repeat from * ending YO, K 5, YO, K 2 tog.

Row 6: Purl.

Row 7: K 2, *YO, K 1, sl 1, K 2 tog, psso, K 1, YO, K 3, repeat from * across ending K 2 instead of K 3.

Row 8: Purl.

Repeat rows 1 through 8 for pattern.

These pattern stitches are merely representative of the many available. Add to them, or play around and come up with your own pattern and texture stitches. It's fun.

13 PATTERN STITCHES FOR CHANGING COLOR

Colors and shades of colors in their infinite combinations, are one of the most exciting elements of fashion. Stimulate your creativeness in selecting new and exciting combinations by having at hand little snips of yarn and/or fabric in different colors and shades of colors.

Lay them on a table. Play around with them, trying different arrangements and rearrangements. You'll know when you have a color combination that's really striking. Before you make your final decision, however, check the colors with your own coloring (hair, eyes, skin) with an eye to enhancing or complimenting what you've got to start with. You may want to keep these little snips for future use in designing for yourself or for others.

This chapter deals with the different ways in which you can use colors in working the knitted fabric. The use of color in trims and finishes is also important.

New Abbreviations: Main Color (MC) Contrasting Color (CC)

TWO-COLOR STRIPES (51)

Just working with the stripe idea, you can develop many variations: stripes within stripes, and alternating narrow and wide stripe arrangements, to name but two.

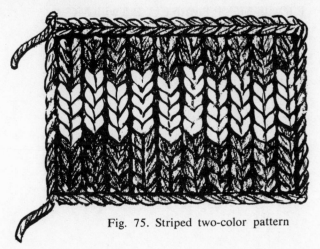

Fig. 75. Striped two-color pattern

75

Cast on 20 sts, with MC.

Work stockinette st for 6 rows ending with a P row.

(Colors must be changed at the beginning of *knit* rows.)

With Contrasting Color (CC) *K 1, slip 1 as if to P, repeat from * across row, resume stockinette stitch for 5 more rows (ending with a P row). Join Main Color (MC) and * K 1, slip 1, repeat from * across row. Work 5 more rows. Bind off.

Note: Stripes may be worked without the slipped st, of course, to make an even line between colors.

GEOMETRIC COLOR KNITTING (52)

Kite-shaped design, used to see how a pattern moves when the color is changed every other row; then, every row (starting with row 14 below). Any design may be worked out using this technique.

Cast on 20 sts, with MC.

Wind one bobbin with MC and one bobbin with CC.

Row 1: K 9, attach CC bobbin, K 2, attach MC bobbin, K 9. Note: To attach bobbin, leave an end and start knitting. The end can be woven in later.

Row 2: P 9, with MC bobbin, P 2 for CC being careful to twist colors to avoid holes, P 9 with MC.

Row 3: K 8 with MC, K 4 with CC, K 8 with MC.

Row 4: Purl rows same as Knit rows.

Row 5: K 7 with MC, K 6, with CC, K 7 with MC.

Row 7: K 6 with MC, K 8 with CC, K 6 with MC.

Row 9: K 5 with MC, K 10 with CC, K 5 with MC.

Row 11: K 4 with MC, K 12 with CC, K 4 with MC.

Row 13: K 3 with MC, K 14 with CC, K 3 with MC.

Row 14: P 4 with MC, P 12 with CC, P 4 with MC.

Row 15: K 5 with MC, K 10 with CC, K 5 with MC.

Row 16: P 6 with MC, P 8 with CC, P 6 with MC.

Row 17: K 7 with MC, K 6 with CC, K 7 with MC.

Row 18: P 8 with MC, P 4 with CC, P 8 with MC.

Row 19: K 9 with MC, P 2 with CC, K 9 with MC.

Row 20: Purl across row with MC. Bind off.

TWO-COLOR CHECKERED PATTERN (53)

This is an example of using two colors in an all-over stitch.

Cast on 19 sts—Multiple of 4 sts plus 3.

Row 1: Using CC, * K 3, sl 1, repeat from * ending K 3.

Row 2: Using CC, * K 3, bring yarn to front of work and sl 1, throw yarn to back of work, repeat from * ending K 3.

Row 3: Using MC, K 1, sl 1, * K 3, sl 1, repeat from * ending K 1.

Row 4: Using MC, K 1, * bring yarn to front of work, sl 1, throw yarn to back of work, K 3, repeat from * ending K 1 instead of K 3.

Repeat these 4 rows for pattern stitch.

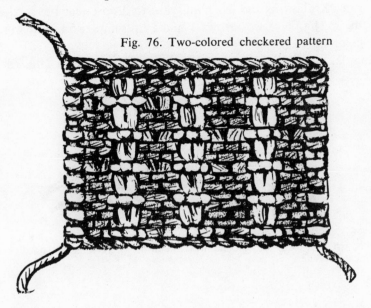

Fig. 76. Two-colored checkered pattern

STRANDING (54)

This sampler, which introduces a new technique, is really given to you so that you can learn to handle two colors in a design, as required by sampler 56 ff.

Cast on 20 sts with MC.

Row 1: K 5, with MC, K 5 with CC, K 5 with MC, K 5 with CC, carrying or stranding the yarn not being worked, loosely across the back of the knitting.

Row 2: P 5 with MC, P 5 with CC, P 5 with MC, P 5 with CC. Repeat these two rows.

WEAVING (55)

This is the best way to handle one or more colors used in a Scandinavian-type color design.

Cast on 20 sts with MC.

Row 1: K 5 with MC, holding CC yarn in left hand with a tension, K allowing the left hand yarn to drop under the st, then over the st (fig. 77); work rows 1 and 2 on sampler 54, weaving as you go along.

Row 2: P, maintaining pattern, weaving as you work (fig. 78).

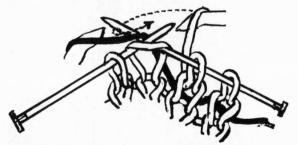

Fig. 77. Color knitting using weaving technique knit row. *Yarn to be carried over the needle, next stitch drop yarn below needle. Repeat from *.

Fig. 78. Color knitting, using weaving technique purl row. *Yarn to be carried over the needle, next stitch drop yarn below needle.

Repeat from *.

SCANDINAVIAN CHART (56)

The design below is the real indication of the superiority of the weaving method. Each square represents 1 stitch and 1 row. Read from the bottom up just as you knit: (fig. 79).
Cast on 24 sts.

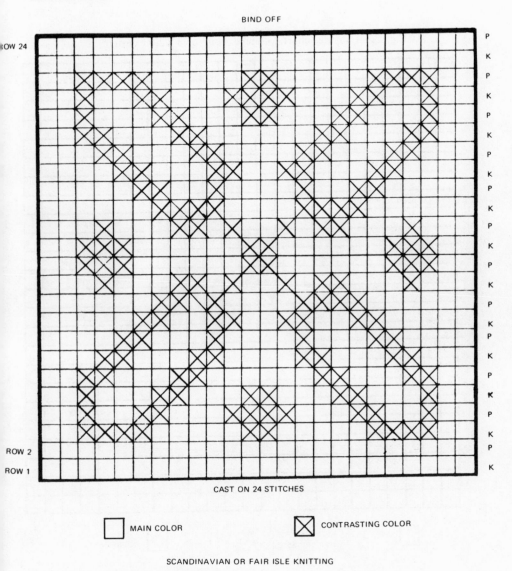

SCANDINAVIAN OR FAIR ISLE KNITTING

Fig. 79. Scandinavian design to work, using weaving method

79

YOUR OWN CHART (57)

Make your own color knitting design chart and knit a sampler from it. It's fun! (Fig. 80.)

Try several colors if you like. Cast on 24 stitches, and work 24 rows with your own design.

Fig. 80. Use this chart to make your own color design.

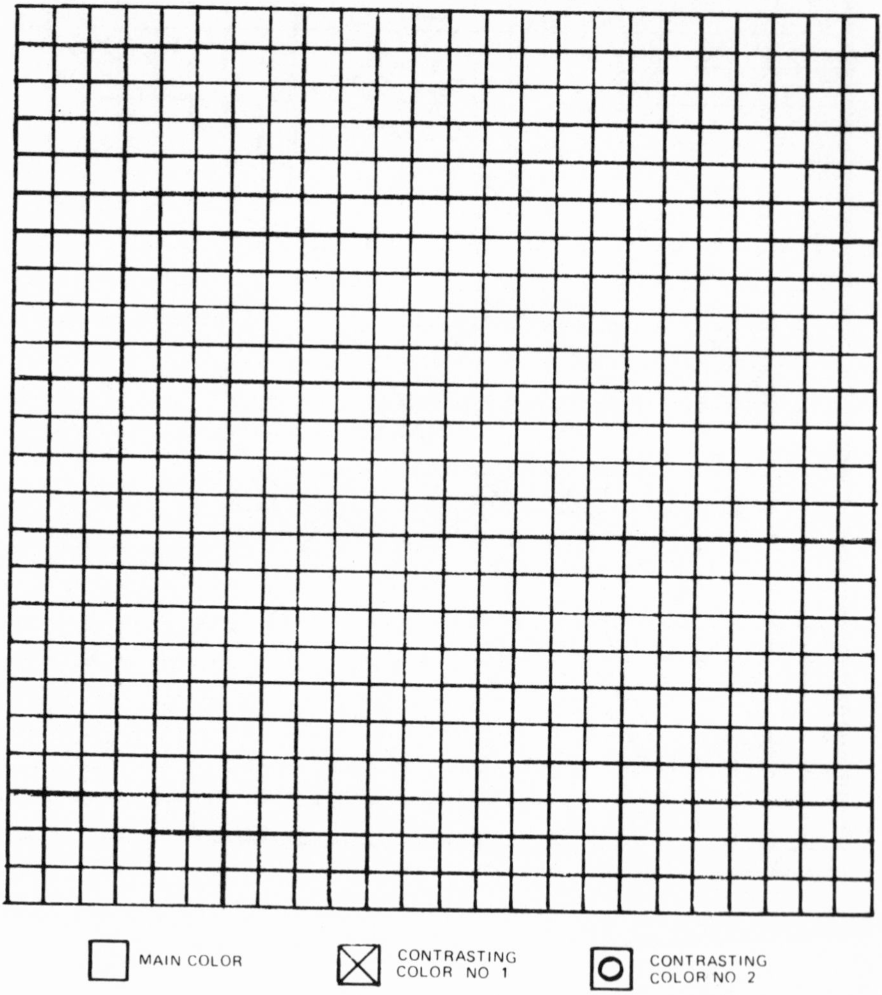

MAIN COLOR   CONTRASTING COLOR NO 1   CONTRASTING COLOR NO 2

80

MOCK PLAID (58)

We can even knit plaid fabrics. Several colors may be used. The horizontal stripes wide or narrow, and the vertical stripes spaced closely or far apart. A lot of room for variation here.

Use two colors MC—Main Color, CC—Contrasting Color. With MC cast on 20 sts. Work stockinette st for 1 inch ending with a purl row. With CC, work 2 rows stockinette stitch. With MC, continue stockinette st for 1 more inch, ending with a purl row. With CC, work 2 rows stockinette stitch. With MC, work 1 more inch in stockinette stitch and bind off. This makes the horizontal stripes.

Complete the plaid by working a vertical stripe an inch apart by using a crochet hook and a double strand of yarn, and working a slip stitch.

Start at the bottom and work the slip stitch loosely.

Fig. 81. Using the mock plaid technique

This is another example of an allover two-color pattern stitch.

Cast on 20 sts with MC. Multiple of 3 sts, plus 2.

Row 1:   (Right side) with CC, K 2, *sl 1, K 2.

Row 2:   With CC, K 2, *yarn in front, sl 1, yarn in back, K 2.

Row 3:   With MC, K 1, *yarn in back, sl 1, K 2 end sl 1, K 2.

Row 4:   With MC, *yarn in front, sl 1, yarn in back, K 2, end yarn in back, K 1.

Row 5:   With CC, *yarn in back, sl 1, K 2, end yarn in back, sl 1, K 1.

Row 6:   With CC, K 1, *yarn in front, sl 1, yarn in back, K 2, end yarn in front, sl 1.

Rows 7 & 8: Repeat Rows 1 and 2 with MC.

Rows 9 & 10: Repeat Rows 3 and 4 with CC.

Rows 11 & 12: Repeat 5 and 6 with MC.

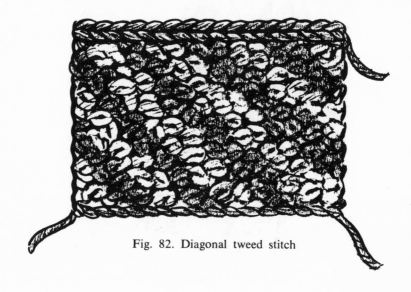

Fig. 82. Diagonal tweed stitch

TWO-TONE CLUSTER STITCH (60)

An unusual stitch because of the technique used.

Multiple of 4 plus 1—With double-pointed needle cast on 21 sts with MC. Use a circular needle in making a knit out of this stitch. Purl Back.

Row 1:   CC *P 1, K 3 tog, hold on needle, YO K same 3 sts tog, slip off needle and repeat from * end P 1. Do not turn. Work Row 2 in same direction as Row 1.

Row 2:   MC. Knit turn.

Row 3:   CC P 2, *K 1, P 3 tog leave on needle, YO P same 3 sts slip off needle, repeat from * end K 1, P 2. Do not turn work. Row 4 is worked in same direction as Row 1.

Row 4:   MC. Purl.

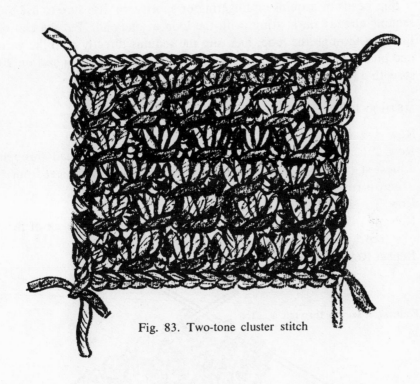

Fig. 83. Two-tone cluster stitch

83

14 SEQUINS, BEADS AND PAILLETTES

The ultimate in elegance in knits can be achieved so easily with sequins or beads worked in as borders or in an allover design.

SEQUIN OR BEAD KNITTING (61)

Slip beads or sequins on fingering or sport yarn. Be sure to use the sequins already on a string, with the loop at one end. Put the end of the yarn through the loop, then slip the sequins directly onto the yarn and push toward the ball of yarn. With the end of the yarn cast on 20 sts with a No. 3 or No. 4 knitting needle.

METHOD 1

Row 1: Purl.

Row 2: K 1, *pull up a sequin and *K sequin or bead through next st (fig. 84), K in back of next st (twist stitch), repeat from * across row, end with a K 1.

Row 3: Purl.

Row 4: K 2, *K sequin or bead through next st, K in back of next st, repeat from * across row.

Repeat Rows 1 through 4 for pattern.

Fig. 84. Knitting a sequin through a stitch

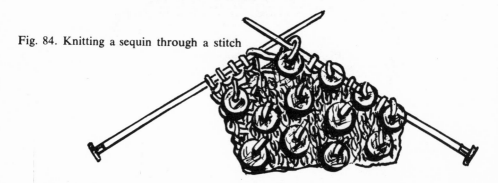

METHOD 2—Cast on 20 sts.

Row 1:   Purl.
Row 2:   *K 1, bring yarn to front of work, sl as to P the next st and
bring sequin or bead to front of this slipped st, repeat from *.
Row 3:   Purl.
Row 4:   K 2 *slip a st, bring sequin or bead to front, K 1, repeat
from * (same method as Row 2).

PAILLETTE KNITTING (62)

Large Sequins

Cast on 20 sts.
Row 1:   Knit.
Row 2:   Purl.
Row 3:   K 2 *holding paillette in front of next st, K 1 st through
hole of paillette, K 3 repeat from * across row.
Row 4:   Purl.
Row 5:   Knit.
Row 6:   Purl.
Row 7:   K 4 *holding paillette in front of next st, K 1 through hole
of paillette, K 3, repeat from *.
Repeat Rows 3 through 7 for pattern.

Fig. 85. Using paillettes on a collar

15   USING NEW PATTERNS AND TEXTURES

Now that you have learned to knit a fabric with different textures and colors you will want to know how to incorporate a different pattern stitch with perhaps a different stitch gauge into existing instructions. First, try the simplest thing: changing the size needle. (If you need more stitches per inch in order to use the same instructions, go to a smaller needle. If you need less stitches per inch, go to a larger needle.) If this is not desirable, or possible, then the following procedure will help you:

STEP 1   Read the instructions, underlining the significant facts as follows:
   a. How many stitches at the waist?
   b. How many stitches at the bust?
   c. How many stitches bound off and/or decreased at armholes?
   d. How many stitches left for the shoulder-to-shoulder measurement, or at the back of the neck, depending on whether it is a set-in sleeve or a raglan-sleeve knit?

STEP 2   Then, make a diagram of the knit instruction as it exists, inserting the number of stitches in the appropriate place. Translate those stitches into inches, using the Gauge Chart in the back of the book.

STEP 3   Make a duplicate diagram of the knit, inserting the inches (which you've just calculated) in the appropriate places, then translate those inches into stitches, again using the new stitch gauge, as shown on fig. 86.

Written Instructions—Back =
            Cast on 100 sts, work until piece measures 12 inches.
Stitch Gauge: At the beginning of *the next two rows bind off 5 sts.*

86

5 sts = 1 in. *Decrease 1 stitch each side every knit row 5 times.*
6 rows = 1 in. *Work even on 80 sts* until armhole measures 8 inches. At the beginning of *the next six rows bind off 9 stitches for shoulders. Bind off* remaining 26 sts.

This method can be used for the entire knit. Where there are fractions involved, extra sts may be necessary or in excess. Remember that the total number of sts taken off at the shoulders, back of neck and under arms must equal the number of sts cast on at the beginning, and that the total number of sts taken off just at the shoulders and the neck must equal the number of sts for the shoulder-to-shoulder measurement.

Determining Size:

How To Be Sure What Size To Select Before Working Knitting Instructions.

Steps 1 and 2 above are helpful in determining what is actually meant by a size 14 or size 16, in terms of inches, in knitting instructions. Before you select a size for yourself, in working a knitting book design, check it by working these first 2 steps. It will save you much time in the long run as well as assure you of greater success.

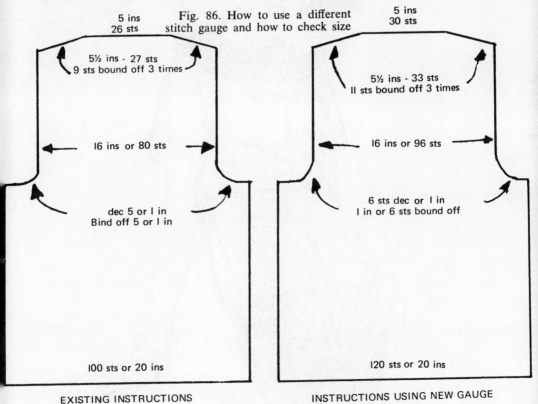

Fig. 86. How to use a different stitch gauge and how to check size

5 ins
26 sts

5½ ins - 27 sts
9 sts bound off 3 times

16 ins or 80 sts

dec 5 or I in
Bind off 5 or I in

100 sts or 20 ins

5 ins
30 sts

5½ ins - 33 sts
II sts bound off 3 times

16 ins or 96 sts

6 sts dec or I in
I in or 6 sts bound off

120 sts or 20 ins

EXISTING INSTRUCTIONS
5 sts = I in
6 rows = I in

INSTRUCTIONS USING NEW GAUGE
6 sts = I in
7 rows = I In

16 TRIMS, EDGINGS AND ORNAMENTS, KNITTED AND CROCHETED

Choosing a trim for a knit and the placement of that trim really brings your creative talents to the fore. These are the touches that convert an ordinary knit into a designer's original.

Fig. 87. Using knitted fringe

There are a variety of ideas here for you to choose from, and you'll want to add even more of your own as you become familiar with the procedures.

KNITTED TRIMS

Tubing (63)

This trim may be used for belts, ties, borders or edgings.
Cast on 5 sts.
Row 1: K 1, *bring yarn to front, slip as to P, bring yarn to back, K 1, repeat from * every row until desired length.

Picot Edge (64)

This edge is appropriate for skirts made from the waist down or tops made from the top down because the trim appears on the bind-off edge.
Cast on 20 sts.
Work stockinette st for 1 inch ending with a P row.
Picot Edge Row: Bind off 2, * cast on 3 on left needle, bind off 7, repeat from * across row.

Fringe (65)

This makes a beautiful collar or trim for almost anything.
Cast on 10 sts.
Row 1: And all rows, *YO, P 2 tog (fig. 88a) every row until

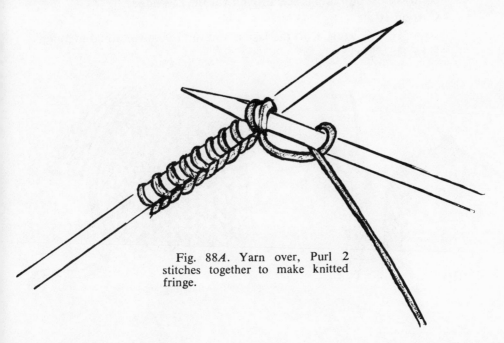

Fig. 88A. Yarn over, Purl 2 stitches together to make knitted fringe.

desired length. Bind off until 2 sts remain. Unravel. See diagram (fig. 88b).

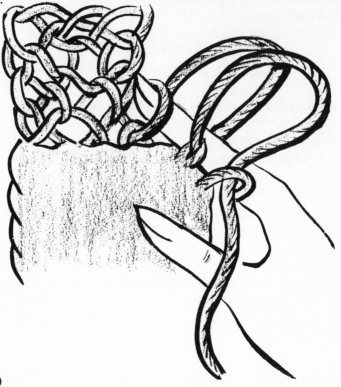

Fig. 88*B*. Unravel

Bias (66)

This makes a very nice conservative trim which may be made in a contrasting color and is sewn right over the raw edges.

Cast on 10 sts.

Row 1: K 2 tog, K to the last st and inc in conventional manner.

Row 2: Purl.

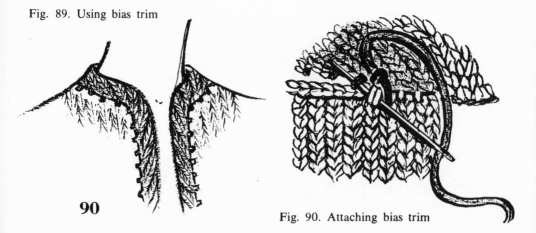

Fig. 89. Using bias trim

90

Fig. 90. Attaching bias trim

Repeat these 2 rows until desired length.

Sew to knitted edge in this manner: With the right and increase side of the bias and the right side of the stockinette sampler facing you, with yarn and yarn needle take one st or 2 strands of the edge and come up through the knot of the increase on the bias. Repeat in this way. Attach the other side of the binding to the inside with a whip stitch.

Note: (a) To be sewn to a stockinette st sampler, 20 sts and worked until square. Steam. (b) Bias may be made with a P row every 5th row or alternating 2 rows of K or 2 rows of P.

Peak Scallop (67)

This trim is begun at the narrow edge. It can be used to trim knits in tiers, or for bordering necklines, fronts, sleeves.

Cast on 4 sts.

Row 1: K 2, yarn over needle twice, K 2 (6 sts).

Row 2: P 2, K 1 in next YO, P 1 in next YO, P 2 (6 sts).

Row 3: Knit.

Row 4: Purl.

Row 5: K 2, yarn over needle twice, K 2 tog, YO needle twice, K 2 (9 sts).

Row 6: P 2, K 1 in next YO, P 1 in next YO, K 1, K 1 in next YO, P 1 in next YO, P 2 (9 sts).

Fig. 91. Using the knitted peak scallop trim

Row 7: Knit.
Row 8: Bind off 5 sts as to purl, P 3 sts (4 sts).
Repeat these 8 rows to form pattern. Work to desired length and bind off.

Scallop (68)

This makes a pretty edging for the bottom of a skirt, dress or blouse. Work it into the sleeves, too.
Cast on 37 sts.
Row 1: Purl.
Row 2: K 1, *K 1 under strand before next st, K 3, K 2 tog, in back of st, K 1, K 2 tog, K 3, K 1 under strand before next st K 1.
Repeat from * across these two rows for pattern.
Scallop may be worked for the entire knit or worked for several inches; then change to the stockinette st.

Bell Pattern (69)

This trim makes a beautiful collar to be sewn on, or a beginning of a sleeve or bottom of a pullover using the purl side of the knit as the right side.
Cast on 20 sts—Multiple of 4 sts plus 4.
Row 1: P 4, *turn, cast on 8 sts using the knitting-on method (see cast-on method), turn, P 4, repeat from * across row.
Row 2: *K 4, P 8, repeat from * across, end K 4.
Row 3: P 4, *K 8, P 4, repeat from * across.
Row 4: *K 4, P 8, repeat from * across row, end K 4.
Row 5: P 4, *slip 1 as if to K, K 1, psso, K 4, K 2 tog, P 4, repeat from * across.
Row 6: *K 4, P 6, repeat from * across row ending with a K 4.
Row 7: P 4, * sl 1 as if to K, K 1, psso, K 2, K 2 tog, P 4, repeat from * across.
Row 8: *K 4, P 4, repeat from * across, end K 4.
Row 9: P 4, * sl 1, K 1, psso, K 2 tog, P 4, repeat from * across.
Row 10: *K 4, P 2, repeat from * across, end K 4.
Row 11: P 4, * K 2 tog, P 4, repeat from * across row.
Row 12: K 4, P 1, repeat from * across, end K 4.

92

Row 13: P 4, P 2 tog, P 3, repeat from * across row, end with a
P 3.
Row 14: K.
Continue stockinette st.

Bell Pattern—Reverse (70)

The reverse Bell Pattern may be used as a ruffle to be sewn on or
worked when picking up stitches, as on a neckline. (The bottom of the
bell is on the bind-off edge rather than the cast-on edge.)
Cast on 20 sts—Multiple of 4 sts plus 4.
Work 3 rows stockinette st, ending with a K row.
Row 1:   *P 4, increase 1 (use lifted increase) repeat from * end
P 4.
Row 2:   *K 4, P 1, repeat from * end with K 4.

Fig. 92. Using the bell pattern

93

Row 3:   *P 4, inc 1, K 1, inc 1, repeat from * end P 4.
Row 4:   *K 4, P 3, repeat from * end K 4.
Row 5:   *P 4, inc 1, K 3, inc 1, repeat from *, end P 4.
Row 6:   *K 4, P 5, repeat from * end K 4.
Row 7:   *P 4, inc 1, K 5, inc 1, repeat from * end P 4.
Row 8:   *K 4, P 7, repeat from * end, K 4.
Row 9:   *P 4, inc 1, K 7, inc 1, repeat from *.
Row 10:   *K 4, P 9, repeat from * end K 4.
Bind off.

Loop Stitch (71)

An entire shell or pullover may be made with this st, or with an inch of plain knitting between each tier of loops.
Cast on 20 sts.
Row 1:   P.
Row 2:   K.
Row 3:   K 1, *insert needle into next st, wind yarn loosely around finger and needle (fig. 93) 3 times and complete K stitch* (4 sts at this point). Repeat between *'s across row, ending with a K 1.
Row 4:   K 1, K across row, knitting 3 loop sts tog; end with a K 1.
Repeat Rows 1 through 4.

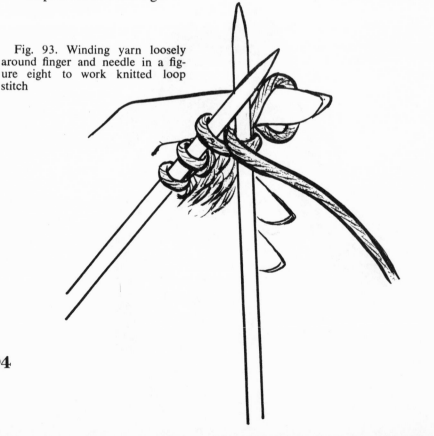

Fig. 93. Winding yarn loosely around finger and needle in a figure eight to work knitted loop stitch

94

Added-on Popcorn (72)

This is particularly useful in applying popcorns of different colors to pick up a color or colors of a skirt. The added-on popcorns may be removed to make the pullover or cardigan a plain one again, so this adds versatility too. They may be scattered or used as borders, clustered to look like grapes. Use your imagination and go on from there.

Apply to a stockinette st sampler. Pull up a loop. K in front and back of loop to get desired number of sts. Begin with 6 sts for a sampler.

Row 1: Purl.
Row 2: Knit.
Row 3: Purl.
Row 4: Knit.
Row 5: P 2 tog across row.
Row 6: K all remaining sts tog. End by pulling yarn through to back of work in the row directly above, and tie.

CROCHETED TRIMS

Tubing (73)

Used for belts, borders, ties and edgings.
Chain 5. Join with a slip st. Work a sc in the top of each chain, then work a sc in each sc around and around until desired length.

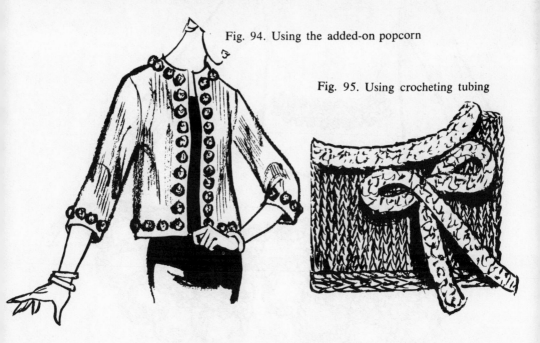

Fig. 94. Using the added-on popcorn

Fig. 95. Using crocheting tubing

Braid (74)

This rather wide braid may be used as a trim for the fronts and cuffs of a knit, down the front of a dress, or used as a half belt for the back or front of a knit.

Loosely ch 23, for a sampler or desired length. Turn. Work a tr crochet in 4th ch from hook and in each ch across. (20 tr crochet and the ch 4 in all,) Turn. Ch. 3, sc in base of the ch 3, * sc in the next 2 sts, ch 3, sc in the same place as beginning of the ch 3. Repeat from * across row and around the other side (the ch side edge).

Large Crochet Trim (75)

Starting at narrow end, ch 11.

Row 1:   Dc in 11th ch from hook. Ch 3, turn.

Row 2:   11 dc in the 11 ch, sp, dc in 4th ch made. Ch 1, turn.

Row 3:   Sc in each dc across and in 3rd st of turning ch (13 sc in all). Turn.

Row 4:   Skip 1 sc, sc in next sc, * ch 5, skip 1 sc, sc in next sc. Repeat from * 4 times more, ending by skipping the next sc, and

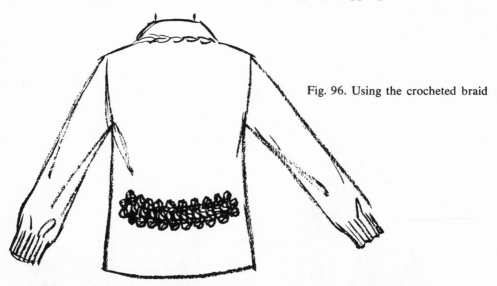

Fig. 96. Using the crocheted braid

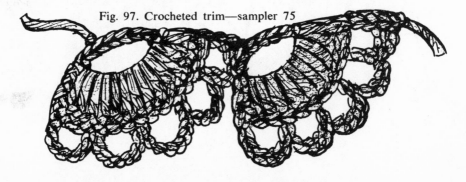

Fig. 97. Crocheted trim—sampler 75

working a dc in the last sc on Ch 10, turn.

Row 5: 1 sc around the ch 5 loop. Ch 3, turn.

Row 6: 11 dc around this new loop, dc in 4th st of ch 10 counting from the st below. Ch 1, turn. Repeat 3rd to 6th rows incl. for desired length, ending with the 4th row.

For more trims, see the next section on "Crocheted Edgings" for edgings that can be made separately and sewn on for trims.

CROCHETED EDGINGS

Crocheted edgings are different from trims in that they can be attached to the knit to finish raw edges. However, some of the following edges can be made separately and sewn on for a trim.

A note to help with some of the following instructions: In making a chain for any length desired, keep in mind that the end of the chain may be cut off without unraveling, so it might be wise to make the chain a little longer than the length desired, so if necessary, a stitch group can be completed.

Simple Crochet Finishing for Knits

In working a crocheted edging around a knit, follow these suggestions: On the sides or raw edges, space the crochet stitches evenly and in such a way as to bring the stretchy raw edges into shape. This means you have to manufacture places to make a stitch. Work 2 or 3 crocheted stitches in each corner. It's important to have the same number of crocheted stitches on each front edge and the same number of crocheted stitches edging the bottom of each sleeve. Don't try to guess by looking, but count stitches to be sure. A crocheted edging may also be used to make raw edges smaller, if necessary, by using a smaller hook and making the stitches farther apart. Very often, necklines and the hem edges of knits need to be made smaller. Using a smaller hook and/or making the stitches farther apart solves this problem.

Shell Stitch (76)

This edging when worked directly on a knit is a pretty way to pull in stretched raw edges. The sampler instructions show it to be worked around a stockinette stitch sampler. It also may be worked separately and sewn on. To make it a separate trim, omit the last sentence and repeat from the Ch 3 until desired length is reached. Ch 3 in corner of knit, *YO, draw up a long loop in base of Ch 3 st.* twice. YO, sl st to lock the 5 loop s. Leave a ½ space, sl st, Ch 3, and repeat between *'s to end of row.

Rickrack (77)

This is an edging that can be made more interesting by lacing ribbon through the base. If this trim is to be worked directly on a knit, work 1 row of sc first.
Ch 26 for a sampler or desired length.
Row 1:   DC in 8th ch from hook. *Ch 2, skip 2 sts of ch, dc in next st, repeat from * across row, ch 5, turn. This forms the base.
Row 2:   DC in 3rd st from hook, 2 dc in same st, *1 dc in next dc, ch 3, 3 dc over dc just made (around the dc post) repeat from * across.

Fig. 98. Using the rickrack edging

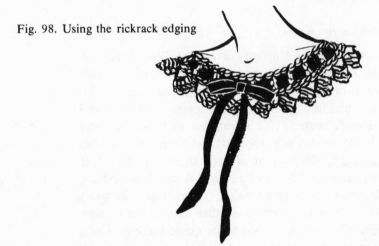

Slant Stitch (78)

This stitch not only makes a pretty edging, and trim, but a pretty fabric, too, for a shell, dress, coat, or even an afghan.
Ch 23 for sampler or chain for desired length. If worked directly on a knit, work 1 row of sc first.

98

Row 1: Work 3 dc in 4th st from hook, skip 3 sts, sl st in next st, *ch 3, 2 dc in same st with sl st, skip 3 sts, sl st in next, repeat from *.

Row 2: Ch 3, turn, 2 dc in sl st, sl st in ch 3 loop of shell of previous row, *ch 3, 2 dc in same sp, sl st in next shell, repeat from * Repeat Row 2 for desired number of times for a wider edging.

If you prefer to use this for a trim, rather than an edging, repeat Row 1 on opposite side of chain.

Fig. 99. Using the slant stitch for a trim

Loop Trim (79)

A ruffle of loops at the neckline and cuffs is a very attractive touch. Add sequins or paillettes and you have something appropriate for evening.

Chain 20. Work 1 row sc, turn.

Loop Row: (Loops appear at the back of the work.) Insert hook into first sc, wind yarn twice around index finger, yarn over hook, then complete a sc and sl yarn off finger, thus forming a loop. For more uniform loops, the yarn can be wrapped around a strip of cardboard ¾ to 1" wide and 3" to 4" long.

Work 1 row sc, then repeat loop row.

Fig. 100. The crocheted loop stitch

Trim or Edging, 1 (80)

Chain 36 for sampler or make a chain slightly longer than desired length.

Row 1:   Work a sc in 2nd ch from hook and in each ch across (35 sc). Ch 1, turn.

Row 2:   Sc in 1st sc, *ch 3, skip 3 sc, 3 tr in next sc holding back on hook the last loop of each tr (4 loops in all). YO hook and pull through all loops making a cluster. Ch 3, work another cluster in the next sc, ch 3, work a third cluster in the next sc, ch 3 (three clusters worked in 3 sc in a row with a ch 3 between them). Now skip 3 sc and work a sc in each of the next 3 sc. Repeat from * ending with a sc in the last sc. Ch 1, turn.

Row 3:   * 3 sc in each of the next 2 sps (around the ch's of the previous row), ch 6, 3 sc in each of the next 2 sps, sc in each of the sc of 3 sc group. Repeat from * across, ending with a sc in the last sc. Ch 1. turn.

Row 4:   *Sc in next 6 sc, in next ch 5 loop make 2 sc, ch 4 and 2 sc; sc in next 6 sc, skip the next 3 sc. Repeat from * across. End it.

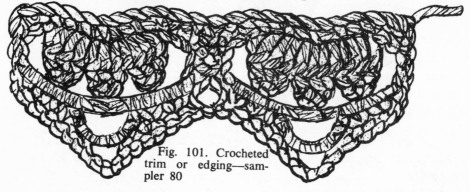

Fig. 101. Crocheted trim or edging—sampler 80

Trim or Edging, 2 (81)

Ch 31 for a sampler or make a chain slightly longer than desired length.

Row 1:   Sc in 2nd ch from hook and in each ch across (number of sc must be a multiple of 10). Ch 5, turn.

Row 2:   *Skip 4 sc, dc in next sc, ch 2, dc in same place, ch 5, skip 4 sc, sc in next sc, ch 5. Repeat from * across, ending with a ch 5, and a sc in the last sc. Turn.

Row 3:   Ch 5, *dc in next ch 2 sp, ch 3, sc in 3rd ch from hook
(picot made), dc in same sp, work a picot and a dc in same sp 2
more times (3 picots and 4 dc's in all), (ch 3, sc in next sp) twice;
ch 3. Repeat from * across, ending with ch 5, sc in last ch. End it.

Fig. 102. Crocheted trim or edging—sampler 81

Trim or Edging, 3 (82)

Make a chain slightly longer than length desired. Ch 23.

Row 1:   Sc in 2nd ch from hook, * ch 5, sc in next 5 ch's. Repeat
from * across until row is length desired ending with ch 5, sc in next
ch (be sure to have an odd number of loops). Ch 1, turn.

Row 2:   Work 2 sc in the first ch 5 loop, *ch 3, make 7 tr in next
ch 5 loop, ch 3, 3 sc in next ch 5 loop. Repeat from * across,
ending with 2 sc in the last ch 5 loop. Ch 1, turn.

Row 3:   Sc in 1st sc, * ch 7, holding back on hook the last loop of
each tr make a tr in each of the next 7 tr (8 loops on hook), yarn
over and draw through all loops on hook, ch 7, skip next sc, sc in
next sc. Repeat from * across ending with sc in last sc. Ch 1,
turn.

Row 4:   *7 sc over next ch 7 loop, ch 7, sc in 7th ch from hook,
7 sc over next ch 7 loop. Repeat from * across. End it.

Fig. 103. Crocheted trim or edging—sampler 82

The beauty of the button-on flower is that it can be added on or taken off. You can have a basic knit and change the design as easily as you can button a button. Color variations can be used here, too. Design your own button-on flower. Just start with a crocheted ring, and use the basic crochet stitches in different combinations. These flowers can also be sewn on for trim.

Button-on Flower with Looped Petals (83)

Ch 5, join with a sl st to form a ring.
Rnd 1:   Work 8 sc in ring.
Rnd 2:   *In next sc, work a sl st, ch 10, sl st twice. Repeat from * Work 2 ch 10 loops in each sc. (16 loops in all.) End it.

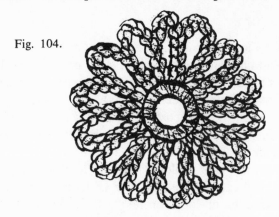

Fig. 104.

Button-on Flower with Curved Petals (84)

Ch 5, join with a sl st to form a ring.
Rnd 1:   Work 10 sc into ring.
Rnd 2:   *Sl st in next sc, ch 6, 1 sl in second ch from hook, 1 sc in next ch, 1 hdc in next ch, 1 dc in each of last 2 ch, 1 sl st as first sl st (1 petal made). Repeat from * in each sc around ring. 10 petals. End it.

Fig. 105.

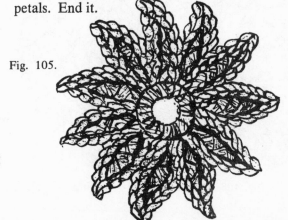

Ruffled Button-on Flower (85)

Ch 5, join to make a ring.

Rnd 1:   Ch 4, *dc, ch 2 in ring, repeat from * 6 times more. Ch 2, and join (9 spaces all together).

Rnd 2:   Ch 5, work 5 tr in the ch 2 space, *fold and work 6 tr around the post of the dc. In next sp, work 6 tr. Repeat from * around, join and end it.

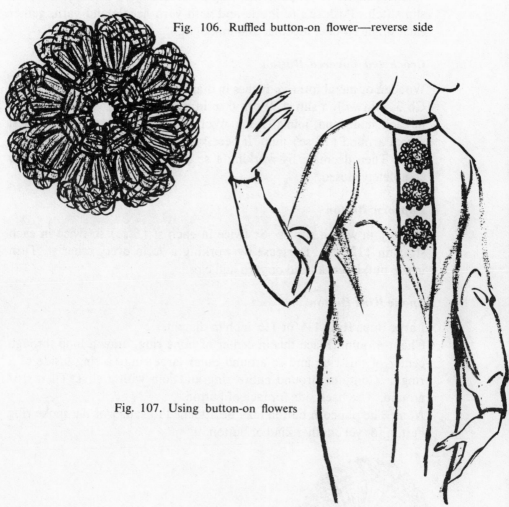

Fig. 106. Ruffled button-on flower—reverse side

Fig. 107. Using button-on flowers

CROCHETED BUTTONS

Buttons can also be used for trim as well as for the function of closing an opening.

Crocheted Bone Ring Button

Bone ring, ⅞ or ¾ inch in diameter.
Work as many sc around bone ring as necessary to cover, join with a slip stitch. Push sc's to inside and with yarn needle and yarn, gather each single crochet together and pull tight.

Crocheted Covered Button

Wooden or metal form ⅞ inches in diameter.
Ch 3, join with a slip st. Work 6 sc in center of ring, join. Work 2 sc in each sc around, join (12 sc). Work 1 sc in next st, 2 sc in next st repeat around (18 sc) join. If necessary to cover form, work 1 round even. Then decrease by working 1 sc in every other sc until form is completely closed.

Popcorn Button

Ch 3, join with a slip st. Sc twice in each st (6 sc) sc twice in each st again (12 sc). Decrease by working a sc in every other st. Turn inside out, insert a bead or yarn and close.

Spoke Ring Button

Large Bone Ring 1¼ or 1½ inch in diameter.
Chain 4, join. Place this in center of bone ring, draw a loop through center of this ring and sc around outer large ring (a ring inside of a ring). Continue around entire ring and join with a sl st. Then sl st around. Use back side for face of button.
Note: The popcorn button may be attached to center of the spoke ring button for yet another kind of button.

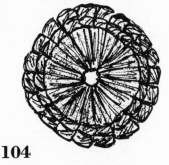

Fig. 108. Spoke ring button

Spider Stitch Button

Use a cardboard form, using the sketch as a pattern, insert the numbers according to the sketch (fig. 111):

1. Take a 3-yard piece of yarn.
2. Thread one end on a yarn needle.
3. Pass the other end through the center hole and hold with thumb on top of form.
4. Wind in sequence 1 — 2 — 3 — 4 — 5 — 6 — 7 — 8, then back to 2.
5. Pass needle under and over stitches at the center to anchor firmly.
6. Back stitch over each spoke (over 2 spokes and under 1 spoke). Work the back stitch counter-clockwise until form is filled.
7. Remove form and draw up end with needle and close around a cotton or yarn stuffing or other form.

Either side may be used for the right side. The spider stitch button and the popcorn button may be used as neckline and sleeve trims on pullovers as well as to button cardigans.

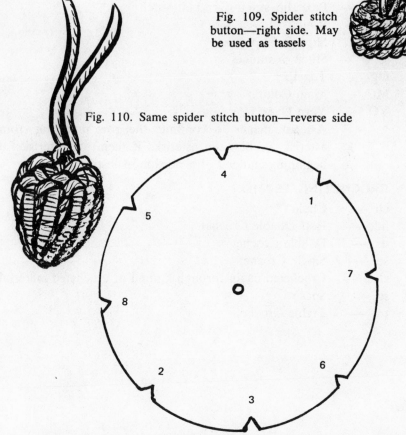

Fig. 109. Spider stitch button—right side. May be used as tassels

Fig. 110. Same spider stitch button—reverse side

Fig. 111. Pattern for cardboard form used to make spider stitch button

GLOSSARY OF TERMS
AND ABBREVIATIONS

KNITTING TERMS:

CC — Contrasting Color
dec — Decrease
inc — Increase
K — Knit
P — Purl
psso — Pass slip stitch over knit stitch
rnd — Round
sl — Slip, or slipped
st(s) — Stitch or stitches
tog — Together
MC — Main Color
YO — Yarn Over
* — Asterisk means to continue the row repeating from the asterisk, or between asterisks if there are asterisks at the beginning and end of a portion of instructions.

CROCHETING TERMS:

ch — Chain
hdc — Half Double Crochet
dc — Double Crochet
sc — Single Crochet
sl st — Crocheted chain through knitted or crocheted material.
sp — Space
trc — Treble Crochet

PART III:
BASIC KNITTING PATTERN
PROJECTS

Now you may wish to begin your project.

Be sure your stitch gauge is the same as the instructions indicate. Always make a sampler, wash it, and let it dry. This is a *must!* Reread the page on Stitch Gauge at the beginning of the book.

The basic project is a raglan cardigan with 4 style variations. The raglan has been selected because of its suitability for most figure types. The first project is a classic cardigan edged with ribbing. The second project is a hemmed cardigan, which may be made longer and become a coat, or third project. The fourth project is a Chanel cardigan, which lends itself to any edging, trim or stitch you may select.

Choose a basic style (the sketches will help you). Decide on a pattern stitch for texture, or on one for color. Then choose your trim and buttons, and all you have left to do is pick the yarn.

Purchasing Yarn

It is most important to get yarn with the same dye lot number. Don't cheat yourself by not getting enough yarn. Most yarn shops and yarn departments take unopened skeins back, but it is very difficult to find more of the exact dye lot if any length of time has elapsed. If knitting worsted or Orlon Sayelle (worsted type) is used, 8 to 10 4-ounce skeins are more than enough to make a cardigan with long sleeves and collar, plus a skirt. If you are in doubt, be guided by instruction books and, of course, by a knowledgeable salesperson.

Reusing Yarns

If you have a hand-knit wardrobe, you also have a storehouse of knitting yarns that can be unraveled and used again

After you unravel the yarn, the kinks can be eliminated by dipping the yarn in cool water. Wind the yarn in hanks as it is being unraveled, tie it in several places before placing it in the cool water, then lay the yarn out to dry. Rewind the yarn into balls and you are ready to start a new fashion with your as-good-as-new yarn.

A custom-spun look can often be achieved by interesting yarn combinations of color, texture and even fiber (machine washable and dryable yarn combined with hand washable yarn). Always make a sampler first, and wash it either by machine or by hand to see what happens, and to know how to care for the finished knit.

17 CLASSIC RAGLAN CARDIGAN WITH RIBBING AND LONG SLEEVES (PROJECT I)

MATERIAL: Knitting Worsted, 5 four-ounce skeins, Orlon Sayelle (worsted type) 5 four-ounce skeins. Mohair or special-blend yarns, 14 40-gram balls or 12 50-gram balls.

SIZES: 32 (34-36-38-40).

Note: A two-inch allowance has been made. Example: If bust measures 36 inches, make size 36, which is designed to be 38 inches around.

GAUGE: 4 stitches = 1 inch, 5 rows = 1 inch.

BACK

With No. 8 needles, cast on 66 (70-74-78-82) stitches. Work K 1, P 1 ribbing for 2 ins. Change to No. 10 needles and work in stockinette st until piece measures 12 inches or desired length. *To Shape Raglan Armhole:* At the beginning of the next two rows bind off 2 sts. Then decrease 1 st each side every knit row (every other row) as follows: K 2 together, work to within 2 sts of end, slip next st as if to K, K last st, then pass slipped stitch over the K st (psso) *or* use full-fashioned decrease method: At beg of dec row, K 1, sl 1 as to K, K 1, psso (pass slip st over K st). K to within 3 sts of end, K 2 tog, K 1.

Fig. 112. Classic basic raglan

Continue stockinette st and decreasing until there are 21 (23-25-27-29) decrease rows or 20 sts remaining. Bind off.

The instructions for the sleeves are given before the fronts so that you have more time to decide what techniques or stitches you wish to use on the fronts.

SLEEVES

With No. 8 needles, cast on 36 (36-38-38-40) sts. Work K 1, P 1 ribbing for 2 ins. Change to No. 10 needles. Work in stockinette st, increasing 1 st each end every inch 6 times (8 times—9 times—11 times—12 times). There will be 48 (52-56-60-64) sts on needle. Work even until piece measures 17 inches or desired length. *To Shape Ralgan Sleeve:* At the beg of next 2 rows bind off 2 sts. Dec 1 st each side every other row (same number of decreases as back, using same decreasing method), until 2 sts remain. Bind off.

LEFT FRONT

With No. 8 needles, cast on 37 (39-41-43-45) sts. Work K 1, P 1 ribbing for 2 inches. Change to No. 10 needles and work in stockinette st (a cable or popcorn design can be inserted, if desired) until piece measures same as back. Bind off 2 sts on arm edge. Then dec 1 st every other row on arm edge until 24 sts remain. *To Shape Neck:* Bind off 6 sts at neck edge. Then dec 1 st at neck edge every other row 4 times, continue dec at arm edge *at the same time.* Continue on arm edge until there are same number of decreases as back or 1 st remaining. Fasten off.

RIGHT FRONT

Same as left front with reverse shaping and knit-in buttonholes if desired, using the left front as a guide.

FINISHING

Crochet or weave seams together. With No. 8 needles pick up stitches around neck and work K 1, P 1 ribbing for 1 inch. If collar is desired, change to No. 10 needles after the 1-inch ribbing and continue in pattern or stockinette stitch until desired length. Bind off loosely.

18 HEMMED RAGLAN CARDIGAN WITH 3/4 LENGTH SLEEVES (PROJECT II)

MATERIAL: Knitting Worsted or Orlon Sayelle (worsted type) 4 four-ounce skeins. Mohair, or special-blend yarns, 12 40-gram balls or 10 50-gram balls.

SIZES: 32 (34-36-38-40). *Note:* A two-inch allowance has been made. Example: If bust measures 36 inches, make size 36, which is designed to be 38 inches around.

GAUGE: 4 stitches = 1 inch, 5 rows = 1 inch.

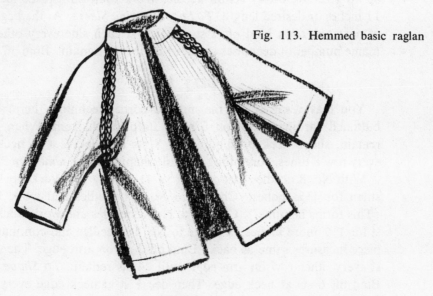

Fig. 113. Hemmed basic raglan

BACK

With No. 8 needles cast on 66 (70-74-78-82) stitches. Work in stockinette stitch for 1½ inches. Change to No. 10 needles and work

1 row (this forms hemline). Change to No. 8 needles and for 1½ more inches work stockinette stitch. (This completes hem.) Change to No. 10 needles and continue in stockinette stitch until piece measures 12 inches above hemline. *To Shape Raglan Armhole:* At the beginning of the next two rows bind off 2 sts. Then decrease 1 st each side every knit row (every other row) as follows: K 2 tog, work within 2 sts of end, slip next st as if to K, K last st, then pass slipped stitch over the K st. (psso). For full-fashioned decrease, see sampler #11. Continue stockinette st and decreasing until there are 21 (23-25-27-29) decrease rows or 20 sts remaining. Bind off.

SLEEVES

With No. 8 needles cast on 38 (42-46-50-54) sts. Work stockinette st for 1½ inches. Change to No. 10 needles and work 1 row. (This forms hemline.) Change to No. 8 needles and continue stockinette st for 1½ more inches. Change to No. 10 needles, continue working stockinette st increasing 1 st each end every inch 5 times. There will be 48 (52-56-60-64) sts on needle. Work even until piece measures 11 inches or desired length. *To Shape Raglan Sleeve:* At the beginning of next two rows bind off 2 sts. Dec 1 st each side every other row (same number of decreases as back) until 2 sts remain. Bind off.

LEFT FRONT

You may want to use the mitered corner technique here. For a buttoned cardigan, cast on 6 more sts on each front. When 30 sts remain, shape neck by binding off 8 sts and dec 1 st at neck edge every row 8 times, continuing armhole shaping *at the same time.*

With No. 8 needles cast on 37 (39-41-43-45) sts. Work stockinette stitch for 1½ inches. Change to No. 10 needles and work 1 row. (This forms hemline.) Change to No. 8 needles and work stockinette st for 1½ more inches. Change to No. 10 needles and continue until piece measures same as back. Bind off 2 sts on arm edge. Then dec 1 st every other row on arm edge until 24 sts remain. *To Shape Neck:* Bind off 6 sts at neck edge. Then dec 1 st at neck edge every other row 4 times, continue dec at arm edge *at the same time.* Continue on arm edge until there are same number of decreases as back, or 1 st remains. Fasten off.

RIGHT FRONT

Same as left front with reverse shaping and knit-in buttonholes if desired, using the left front as a guide.

FACING

A facing strip may be made afterwards, instead of being worked into the knit, by casting on 8 sts, and working stockinette st same length as fronts and sewn on with a sc edging. Make two. Be sure facing draws in front edges to match length in front center.

NECK FINISHINGS

Neck sts may be picked up and worked in stockinette or a reverse stockinette stitch for 3 inches. Bind off loosely and turn to inside and attach with a whip stitch, or neck sts may be picked up and worked in ribbing.

19 HEMMED BASIC RAGLAN COAT WITH FULL-LENGTH SLEEVES (PROJECT III)

MATERIAL: 8 4-ounce skeins of either knitting worsted or Orlon Sayelle (worsted type), used together with 24 40-gram balls or 20 50-gram balls of either mohair or special blend yarns. Using this blend creates the fabric firmness best suited to a full-length coat.

SIZES: 32 (34-36-38-40). *Note:* A 2-inch allowance has been made, as follows: If bust measures 36 inches, make size 36, which is designed to be 38 inches around. This unbuttoned coat made with the two-inch allowance works out perfectly if the coat is to be worn over dresses. If it is intended to be worn over suits, move up to the *next* size, which would be size 38, which permits a 4-inch allowance.

GAUGE: 4 stitches = 1 inch; 5 rows = 1 inch.

BACK

With No. 8 needles and knitting worsted only, cast on 66 (70-74-78-82) stitches. Work in stockinette stitch for 1½ inches. (This completes underside of hem.) At this point, continue with same size needle and worsted, but add your second strand of yarn, using the two strands as if they were one. Continue with the two strands throughout. Continue using stockinette stitch until piece measures desired length (as per your own measurements). *To shape raglan armhole:* At the beginning of the next two rows, bind off 2 stitches. Then decrease 1 stitch each side every knit row (i.e., every other row), as follows: K 2 tog, work until within 2 sts of end; slip next st as if to K; K last st; then pass slipped stitch over the K st (psso). (For full-fashioned decrease, see sampler 11.) Continue stockinette st and decreasing until there are 21 (23-25-27-29) decrease rows or 20 sts remaining. Bind off.

114

SLEEVES

With No. 8 needles and knitting worsted only, cast on 38 (42-46-50-54) sts. Work stockinette st for 1½ inches. With same size needles, worsted, and the second strand of yarn, continue stockinette st, increasing 1 stitch each end every 2 inches 5 times. There will be 48 (52-56-60-64) sts on needle. Work even until piece measures 14 inches or desired length. *To shape raglan sleeve:* At the beg of next 2 rows, bind off 2 sts. Dec 1 st each side every other row (same number of decreases as back) until 2 sts remain. Bind off.

LEFT FRONT

The facings are made separately and sewn on. This prevents the sagging often seen on full-length coats. (See Facing instructions below.) With No. 8 needles and knitting worsted alone, cast on 37 (39-41-43-45) sts. Work stockinette st for 1½ inches. With same size needle and 2 strands of yarn, continue in stockinette st until piece measures same as back. Bind off 2 sts on arm edge. Then dec 1 st every other row on arm edge until 24 sts remain. *To shape neck:* Bind off 6 sts at neck edge. Then dec 1 st at neck edge every other row 4 times; continue dec at arm edge *at the same time.* Continue on arm edge until there are same number of decreases as on back, or until 1 st remains. Fasten off.

RIGHT FRONT

Same as left front, with reverse shaping.

Facing (Make 2)

Use No. 8 needles and both strands. Make a facing strip by casting on 8 stitches. Work stockinette st 1½ inches less than the length of the fronts. Attach the facing strip after you've sewn the underside of the hem, starting it just above the turned-under part of the hem. This avoids any unnecessary thicknesses. The facing strip may be attached by using a single crochet st through both coat and facing, or you may use the weaving method, then turning the strip under and sewing with a whip stitch. Be sure that the facing brings the stretched raw edges back to the proper length.

115

NECK FINISHINGS

With No. 8 needles and the 2 strands of yarn, pick up neck stitches and work stockinette st for 3 inches. Bind off loosely and fold over to inside. Attach with a whip stitch.

20 PLAIN CHANEL BASIC RAGLAN SLEEVE CARDIGAN (PROJECT IV)

MATERIAL: 4 4-ounce skeins of knitting worsted or Orlon Sayelle (worsted type). 12 40-gram balls or 10 50-gram balls of mohair or special-blend yarn.

SIZES: 32 (34-36-38-40). *Note:* A two-inch allowance has been made. Example: If bust measures 36 inches, make size 36, which is designed to be 38 inches around.

GAUGE: 4 stitches = 1 inch, 5 rows = 1 inch.

BACK

With No. 10 needles, cast on 66 (70-74-78-82) stitches. Work in stockinette stitch until piece measures 12 inches or desired length. *To Shape Raglan Armhole:* At the beginning of the next two rows, bind off 2 sts. Then decrease 1 st each side every knit row (every other row) as follows: K 2 together, work to within 2 sts of end, slip next st as if to K, K last st, then pass slipped stitch over the K st (psso). For

Fig. 114. Chanel basic raglan

full-fashioned decrease, see sampler 11. Continue stockinette st and decreasing until there are 21 (23-25-27-29) decrease rows or 20 sts remaining. Bind off.

SLEEVES

Cast on 38 (42-46-50-54) sts. Increase 1 st each end every inch 5 times. There will be 48 (52-56-60-64) sts on needle. Work even until piece measures 11 ins or desired length. *Shape Raglan Sleeve:* At the beg of next 2 rows bind off 2 sts, dec 1 st each side every other row (same number of decreases as back) until 2 sts remain. Bind off.

LEFT FRONT

For a buttoned cardigan, cast on 6 more sts on each front. When 30 sts remain, shape neck by binding off 8 sts and dec 1 st at neck edge every row 8 times, continuing armhole shaping *at the same time.*

Cast on 37 (39-41-43-45) sts. Work even in stockinette st (a cable or popcorn design can be inserted if desired) until piece measures same as back. Bind off 2 sts on arm edge. Then dec 1 st every other row on arm edge until 24 sts remain. *Shape Neck:* Bind off 6 sts at neck edge. Then dec 1 st at neck edge every other row 4 times, continue dec at arm edge *at the same time.* Continue decreasing on arm edge until there are same number of decreases as back or 1 st remains. Fasten off.

RIGHT FRONT

Same as left front with reverse shaping and knit-in buttonholes if desired, using the left front as a guide.

FINISHING

Assemble with a slip stitch, or the weaving method, and finish as desired. If a sc edging is preferred, start at bottom of right front on right side of work; with size G crochet hook, work 1 row sc around fronts, neck and bottom of sweater. Row 2: Mark for buttonholes on right front and work sc in each st, then skip 3 sc where buttonholes are desired, then continue sc in each st around. Row 3: Sc in each st and ch 3 over the skipped 3 sc on previous row. Rows 4 and 5, sc in each st around. Work 5 rows sc on each sleeve.

118

PART IV:
CHARTING AND
DESIGNING

CHARTING INDIVIDUAL MEASUREMENTS

	Body	Favorite Garment	Finished
NECK			
BUST			
WAIST			
HIP			
LENGTH FROM WAIST			
TO UNDERARM			
SHOULDER TO SHOULDER			
WIDTH OF UPPER			
ARM			
WIDTH OF LOWER			
ARM			
WRIST			
LENGTH FROM WRIST			
TO UNDERARM			
ARMHOLE AROUND CURVE			
TO SHOULDER TIP			
SKIRT LENGTH			
HIP TO WAIST			
STITCH GAUGE			
ROW GAUGE			

Determining Finished Measurements

Because we all have different ideas as to fit and style, depending on our type of figure and what feels comfortable, finished measurements must be determined individually rather than according to a set of rules. To help you do this, here are three steps to consider.

STEP 1: Insert your actual body measurements in column 1.

STEP 2: Take the measurements of a dress, suit or coat whose fit you like. It doesn't have to be a knit. Enter it in column 2.

STEP 3: Before you fill in the last column, take the tape-measure test. Hold the tape measure around you at the finished measurement you think will be best. Know that the way the tape measure feels at the various measurement points is the way the knit will feel, then if necessary, make adjustments. Fill in the third column, "Finished" after the adjustments. Now you are ready to design and chart.

Knit to Finished Measurements Only.

21 SKIRTS

The firmer the knit, the better the fit, particularly in skirts, coats and dresses, where there is more strain on the fabric. It is wise to make samplers with different size needles to determine which will give maximum firmness to the knit you plan to make.

The following stitch gauge and measurements are used throughout as examples:

Finished Measurements
Used for Examples

5 sts = 1 inch, 6 rows = 1 inch

Neck	15 inches
Bust	36 inches
Waist	26 inches
Hip	36 inches
Length from Waist to Underarm	8 inches
Shoulder to Shoulder	15 inches
Width of Upper Arm	13 inches
Width of Lower Arm	10 inches
Wrist	9 inches
Length from Wrist to Underarm	16 inches
Armhole Around Curve to Shoulder Tip	18 inches
Skirt Length	25 inches
Hip to Waist	8 inches

So as to be more sure of yourself in charting to your personal measurements, you may wish to rechart each of the examples given, but translate the figures to a different stitch gauge. This clarifies many questions. A suggested stitch gauge to use for practice is 6 sts = 1 inch, 7 rows = 1 inch. It is easier to check your answers in this way, and will give you more confidence in charting to your personal measurements. Use the Rapid Gauge Chart in the back of the book. More errors occur because of a mistake in arithmetic than for any other reason. The chart will eliminate that possibility. Re-reading section 15 ("Using New Patterns and Textures") will also be helpful.

Note that throughout the skirt examples, stitches are mentioned as being decreased or increased. This is to remind you that any skirt style may very easily be worked from the hem to the waist, or conversely, from the waist to the hem.

SKIRTS WITH SIDE SEAMS

Finished measurements to be used on all examples:

Waist	26 inches
Hip	36 inches
Length	25 inches
Length from Waist to Hip	8 inches

Stitch Gauge Used: 5 sts = 1 inch, 6 rows = 1 inch

Skirt 1—Straight Skirt

This first skirt is made in two equal parts, front and back. Make a diagram of the front and the back, insert the inches needed in the appropriate places, and translate the inches into stitches using the Gauge Chart in the back of the book. The inches in the front and back total the finished measurements.

Note: Round out the number of sts to an even number when necessary.

Fig. 115. Straight skirt with side seams: front and back

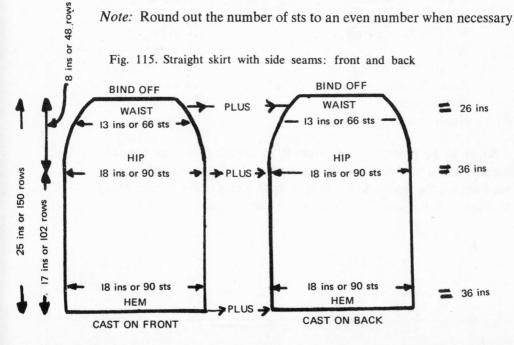

The difference between the waist stitches and the hip stitches then have to be decreased if you are working from the hem to the waist, or increased if you are working from the waist to the hem. The finishing you select will determine how you will actually work the skirt (bottom up or top down). Make a sketch showing how you plan to work the skirt; this will prevent confusion.

If working from the waist to the hem, make a sketch like this:

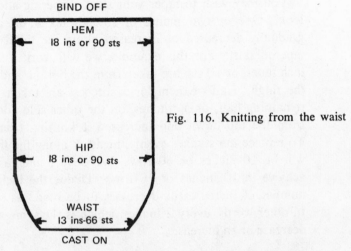

BIND OFF

HEM
18 ins or 90 sts

Fig. 116. Knitting from the waist

HIP
18 ins or 90 sts

WAIST
13 ins-66 sts

CAST ON

In our example there is a 24-stitch difference between the hip and the waist. One half (or 12) may be decreased or increased on one side, and the remaining half, or 12, decreased or increased on the other side. To determine how to work the decreases or increases, divide the number of rows available by the number of decreases or increases to be made. Using our example (fig. 117), your calculations would work out as follows:

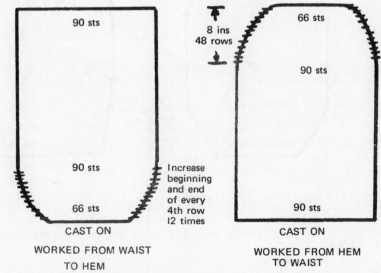

90 sts

8 ins
48 rows

66 sts

90 sts

90 sts

Increase
beginning
and end
of every
4th row
12 times

66 sts

90 sts

CAST ON

CAST ON

WORKED FROM WAIST
TO HEM

WORKED FROM HEM
TO WAIST

Fig. 117. Shaping side seams from the waist and from the hem

	4 rows	or every 4th row a
12 dec.	⌈ 48 rows	decrease or increase
or inc.		may be worked

Now chart your own skirt, using your personal measurements.

Skirt 2—Tapered Skirt

You may wish to taper your skirt. Tapering adds to the long, lean look. One or two inches of stitches taken off at the bottom and gradually decreased or increased along the thigh, produces a nicely tapered skirt. For this example, we will work a 2-inch taper. A 2-inch taper, or 10 sts, are taken from the bottom and added again along the thigh. Half of them, or 5 stitches, are taken from one side, the remaining half, or 5 stitches, on the other side (decreased if knitting from the top down and increased if knitting from the bottom up). To replace the stitches evenly, measure along the thigh. Our example will be 10 inches or 60 rows. We have 5 increases or decreases to achieve in 10 inches or 60 rows. Divide the inches or rows by the number of increases or decreases to be made as shown on fig. 118. In other words, every 2 inches, which is the same as 12 rows, work a decrease or an increase.

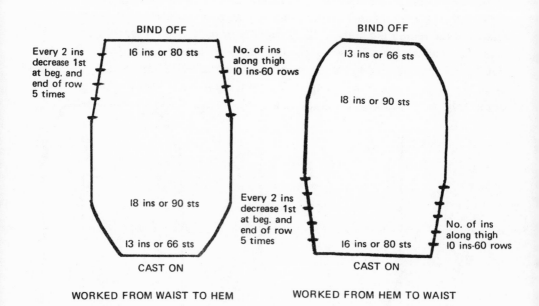

Fig. 118. Tapered skirt, from the waist and from the hem

Skirt 3—Flared or A-Line Skirt

You may wish to have a flared or A-line skirt. The flare may be slight or full. Decide how many more inches of stitches you would like around the bottom of your skirt. For our example, let us add an 8-inch flare, four inches in the front and four inches in the back.

The added 4-inch flare gives us 20 more stitches at the hem than needed at the hip. These 20 stitches then need to be decreased or increased 10 (one half) on one side, and 10 (the other half) on the other side. To decrease or increase them evenly in the length available between the hem and the hip, divide the rows by the number of decreases or increases to be made (see fig. 119).

$$\begin{array}{r} \underline{10 \text{ with } 2 \text{ rows remaining}} \\ 10 \text{ dec.} \quad \underline{102 \text{ rows}} \\ \text{or inc.} \quad \underline{100} \\ 2 \end{array}$$

This means there will be a decrease or increase worked at the beginning and end of every 10th row, with 2 rows left over. These 2 extra rows may be left at the bottom. (K 12 rows first, decrease, then decrease every 10th row if working from the hem to the waist.) If working *from the waist to the hem,* increase every 10th row, with 12 rows remaining as shown in fig. 118.

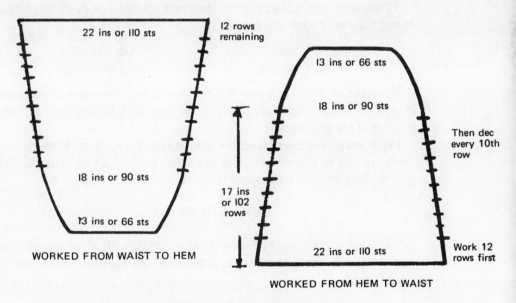

WORKED FROM WAIST TO HEM

WORKED FROM HEM TO WAIST

Fig. 119. A-line or flared skirt, from the waist and from the hem

125

Adding a Dart

Let's take the upper portion of either the flared or straight skirt as our example. In order to shape, we must increase (or decrease, depending on whether we're working from the top down or from the bottom up) a total of 48 stitches—24 in front, 24 in back. Of these 24 back stitches, 12 must be taken off each side. We'll work 6 of these 12 into 2 darts (for placement, see below). The other 6 stitches will be decreased or increased at the side. The same procedure is followed for the front.

The measurement from the hip to the waist is 8 inches. Make the dart half the length, or 4 inches. Translate these inches to rows.

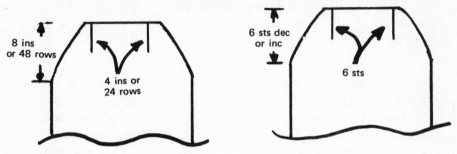

Fig. 120. Adding a skirt dart

To figure the placement of the dart and side decreases or increases, divide the rows by the stitches.

	8th row		4th row
6 sts	48 rows-sides	6 sts	24 rows-darts

Decrease or increase every 8th row for sides. Decrease or increase every 4th row for darts. Begin darts 24 rows or 4 inches from the beginning of the hip shaping.

Darts may be placed near the side seams, or midway between the center of the front or back, and the sides, depending on what would give the best fit. See *Charting a Dress With Darts* for details.

CIRCULAR SKIRTS

This skirt style is worked on a circular needle with all of the stitches cast on at one time, and the decreasing or increasing worked evenly around, eliminating side seams. This skirt may be worked from the hem or from the waist. In our example, we work from the waist first. A circular skirt lends itself very well to a ribbing or pleated effect. In our example, we will use a flared skirt. The hem will have 12 more inches of stitches than the hip and we will use a rib pattern. Always keep in mind the kind of line and shaping that would enhance your figure. Make a sketch of a circular skirt. Insert the inches desired and translate the inches into stitches. It is easier to figure decreases or increases by thinking in "groups of stitches" or multiples, and then rounding out the number of stitches to be cast on. So it will be a multiple of 10, 12 stitches, etc. In our example, the number of stitches cast on is a multiple of 10 stitches.

Because you are going to work in a rib, you will also need to determine the combination of knit and purl stitches (i.e., the kind of rib you want). The number of stitches to be cast on can help you decide.

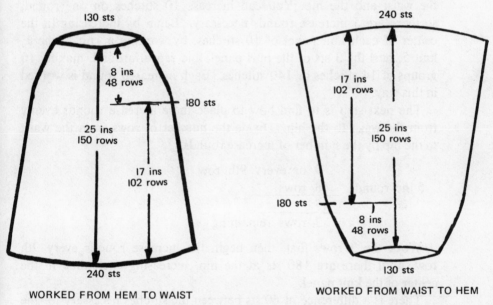

WORKED FROM HEM TO WAIST

WORKED FROM WAIST TO HEM

Fig. 121. Flared circular skirt, from the hem and from the waist

Waist 26 inches or 130 sts. Hip 36 inches or 180 sts, plus 12 inches more at hem, totals 48 inches, or 240 stitches, as shown on fig. 121.
Gauge 5 sts—1 inch
         6 rows—1 inch

Here's an example of thinking in "groups of stitches", or multiples, to determine increasing or decreasing evenly on the round and also to help determine the combination of knit and purl stitches for a rib.

There are 130 stitches on the needle at the waist in your circular skirt example. Another way to state this is that there are 10 groups of 13 stitches. You can increase one stitch in each of the 10 groups (10 stitches increased evenly around) from 130 to 140, 150, 160 on up to the number of stitches needed at the hip.

To determine the rib, for example, let's say that in each group of 13 stitches you want 10 of the stitches to be knit and 3 of the stitches purled. Any combination is possible.

To increase in each of the 10 groups from 13 to 14 stitches on up, you will increase in the center only of each K panel and keep the P 3 the same.

There is a difference of 50 stitches that must be increased between the waist and the hip. You can increase 10 stitches on one round, so there are 5 increase rounds necessary. Begin by increasing in the center of each knit panel of 10 stitches, by working a knit 5, inc 1, knit 5, purl the 3 sts of the purl panel, and repeat around, making 10 groups of 14 stitches or 140 stitches. Each increased round is worked in this way.

The next step is to find how to place these increase rounds evenly from the waist to the hip. Divide the number of rows from the waist to the hip by the number of increase rounds.

$$
\begin{array}{r}
9 \text{ or every 9th row} \\
5 \text{ inc. rounds } \quad \underline{48 \text{ rows}} \\
\underline{45} \\
3 \text{ rows remaining}
\end{array}
$$

Work the 3 rows first, then begin the increase rounds every 9th row, until there are 180 sts at the hip, increasing each time in the center of the knit panel.

There is a difference of 60 sts between the stitches necessary for the hip and the stitches necessary for the hem. Figure the placement of the increase rounds in the same way. There are 102 rows to increase 60 sts or 6 increase rounds. Divide the rows by the rounds needed.

$$
\begin{array}{r}
17 \text{ or every 17th row} \\
6 \text{ inc. rounds } \quad \underline{102 \text{ rows}}
\end{array}
$$

128

In working this skirt from the hem to the waist, reverse the procedure. Any combination of knit or purl stitches may be used, or you may want a plain stockinette stitch skirt. The stitches may be increased or decreased in any number or combinations according to the effect desired.

Select the yarn, a color, a stitch, a style and a length (a long evening skirt may make just the addition to your knit wardrobe that you need) and select a finish.

FINISHING THE TOP OF THE SKIRT

The top of a skirt may be finished in these three ways:

1. With a small hem to be turned down, enclosing an elastic. Not binding off, but whipping down each open stitch over the enclosed elastic will add flexibility.
2. With a crochet: "beading," worked just inside the waist by slipping 1 at the top, ch 5, slip 1, an inch over and below the top, ch 5 and inserting the elastic afterwards.
3. With a "beading" worked on top of the waistline. Work a slip st, ch 5, *dc a half inch over, ch 3, repeat from *, insert elastic.

The kind of finishing and hem selected may add extra inches to the length, and you must adjust accordingly.

Rechart each of these skirts using the same number of inches but translating the inches to a stitch gauge of 6 sts = 1 inch, 7 rows = 1 inch.

Then design and chart a skirt for yourself, using your own measurements. Use a tape measure to decide on the finished measurements you would like for yourself.

22 CAPELETS OR PONCHOS

CHARTING A CIRCULAR CAPE OR PONCHO

Three basic measurements are needed:
1. Finished neck measurement. (If collar, or edging, is to be added, subtract the added inches this may give. In other words, your neck measurement would be larger before the neck finishing.)
2. Finished width at the bottom.
3. Length from the neck to the bottom.

This first example will be a capelet or poncho that slips over the head and is worked on a circular needle. When deciding on your personal finished measurements, always take the tape measure test and know you will need the neck opening large enough to slip over your head and hairdo easily and large enough at the bottom to have free arm movement. For a long cape or poncho, you may make slits for the arms near the elbow by adding another ball of yarn and working back and forth for 8 or 10 inches (to maintain the slits), then join and knit on the round again.

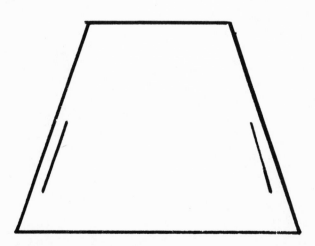

Fig. 122. Circular capelet or poncho, from the hem and from the neck

EXAMPLE

Neck	32 inches
Width at bottom	56 inches
Length	20 inches

Stitch Gauge: 5 sts = 1 inch, 6 rows = 1 inch

Fig. 123. Armhole slit for long cape or poncho

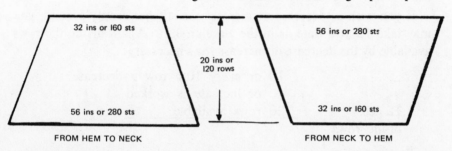

32 ins or 160 sts

56 ins or 280 sts

20 ins or 120 rows

56 ins or 280 sts

32 ins or 160 sts

FROM HEM TO NECK

FROM NECK TO HEM

Decreases or increases may be made evenly around as on the circular skirt (fig. 123) or worked along each arm edge. In this example we will work the increases or decreases along each arm edge. At each arm edge we will place a marker and decrease or increase 1 st before the marker and 1 stitch after the marker, so that 4 stitches will be increased or decreased on 1 row: fig. 124.

Fig. 124. Placing markers for arm-edge shaping on cape

dec or inc
marker
dec or inc

dec or inc
marker
dec or inc

There is a difference of 120 stitches between the neck and the bottom so we have 120 stitches to decrease or increase in 120 rows,

131

or for a 20-inch length. If we decrease or increase 4 stitches at a time, then we need 30 decrease or increase rows. Divide the number of rows we actually have by the number of decrease or increase rows needed:

$$\frac{120 \text{ rows available}}{30 \text{ dec.}} \quad \frac{4 \text{ or every 4th row a decrease or}}{\text{increase is worked}}$$

or inc. rows

If you wish to decrease or increase the stitches evenly around, you may take 10 at a time as in the circular skirt. Again divide the rows available by the decrease or increase rows necessary:

$$\frac{120 \text{ rows available}}{12 \text{ dec.}} \quad \frac{10 \text{ or every 10th row a decrease}}{\text{or increase is worked}}$$

or inc. rows

To increase evenly around on a plain stockinette stitch, it is easier to think of 160 stitches as 10 groups of 16 stitches which need to be increased to 10 groups of 17, then 18, then 19 and so on up to 28 stitches each, for a total of 280 stitches. To begin the increasing, make 2 stitches out of every 16th stitch, using whatever increase method you prefer. To decrease, reverse the process. Think of 280 stitches as being 10 groups of 28 stitches, which will be decreased to 10 groups of 27 (work every 27th and 28th stitch together to begin). Then continue to decrease 1 more stitch in each group as that there will be 26, then 25 on down to 16, or 160 stitches altogether.

CHARTING A BUTTONED CAPELET

To design a buttoned capelet, split the middle of the front and work on straight needles, or back and forth on a circular needle (circular needles accommodate more stitches) and add stitches for the button overlap.

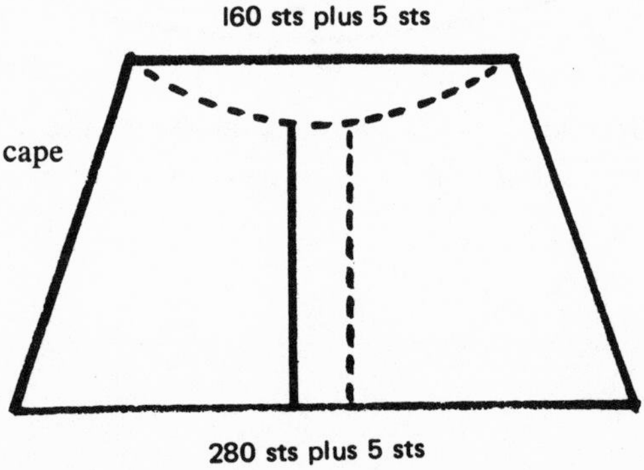

160 sts plus 5 sts

Fig. 125. A buttoned cape

280 sts plus 5 sts

132

23 RAGLANS: PULLOVERS, CARDIGANS AND DRESSES

Raglans are known, and popular, for their easy fit. You may work them in three ways: first, on a circular needle, from the neck down, in one piece; second, on straight needles, in separate sections; third, a combination, using straight needles in part for sections, but working the top, or yoke, in one piece. The first or entirely circular method offers several advantages: you have more freedom to use color designs, as you don't need to worry about carrying the design from one section to another; in addition, you can incorporate a variety of pattern stitches and finishes. The indispensable ingredient is imagination!

This first example will be a raglan made in sections. The back will be the same for a pullover or a cardigan. The stitch gauge: 5 sts = 1 inch, 6 rows = 1 inch.

The finished measurements used are:

Bust	36 inches
Hip	36 inches
Neck	17 inches
Raglan length (Measure from the back of the neck straight down to a line where the underarm shaping begins.)	10 inches
Wrist (The finished wrist measurement should be approximately 2 inches more than the actual wrist measurement, so as to fit over the hand.)	9 inches
Upper Arm	13 inches
Hip to Underarm	14 inches

133

BACK

Half the total bust or hip measurement becomes the back measurement and the other half, the front measurement. (In working your own raglan, if the raglan comes to the hip and the hip measurement is larger than the bust, use the hip measurement. If the bust is larger, use the bust measurement. You may increase from a small hip to a larger bust, but never decrease from a larger hip to a smaller bust, this procedure would accentuate the large hip and small bust.)

We proportion the stitches for the neck and armhole by dividing the total number of back stitches into thirds. One third for the back of the neck; decrease the remainder on each side. (These proportions may be varied according to style or when necessary to make a compromise between the raglan length and the number of stitches to be decreased within that length.)

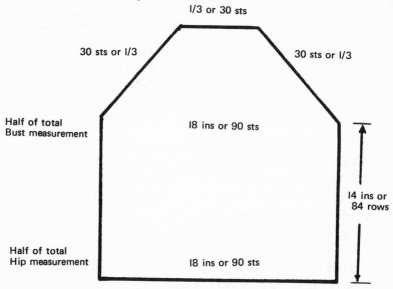

Fig. 126. Proportioning stitches for a raglan back

If the raglan length is 10 inches and we have a 6-rows, 1-inch gauge, we then have 60 rows in which to decrease 30 stitches on each side. The decreases are worked at the beginning and end of each knit row. Purl rows are worked even. Two rows are then used for each

134

decrease row. 60 rows, to achieve 30 decreases each side every knit row, will fit in perfectly.

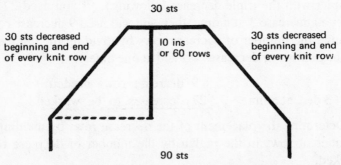

Fig. 127. Decreasing for a raglan shaping

How to vary proportions when stitches to be decreased and rows available do not work out perfectly:

If you have 30 decreases to make on each side and want to maintain a 9-inch raglan instead of a 10-inch raglan and therefore only have 54 rows to decrease in, work it like this: Find the number of decreases that *can* be worked into 54 rows decreasing every knit row by dividing 54 by 2 or 27 decreases. The extra 3 sts on each side may then be bound off at the beginning of the raglan shaping; fig. 128.

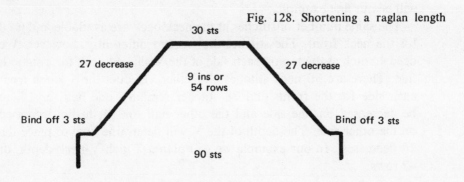

Fig. 128. Shortening a raglan length

If you don't have enough stitches to be decreased at the beginning and end of every knit row in the raglan length necessary, you may first check whether you can use a shorter raglan length and still maintain a good fit. If you cannot, you may add some extra stitches to the back of the neck. Or, you may work a triple decrease (3 stitches decreased at each side at one time). See Sampler 12 (double decrease sampler with the triple decrease following). If you need 27 decreases and you decrease 3 at a time, then you will need 9 decrease rows. (Determine the number of decrease rows by dividing the number of rows by the number of decreases worked at one time.)

$$\begin{array}{r} 9 \text{ decrease rows needed} \\ \text{3 dec. at a time} \quad \overline{27 \text{ decreases to be worked}} \end{array}$$

Determine the placement of the decrease rows by dividing the total number of rows in the raglan by the number of decrease rows to be worked.

$$\begin{array}{r} 6 \text{ or every 6th row a triple decrease may be worked} \\ \text{9 dec. rows} \quad \underline{60 \text{ rows in raglan length}} \\ \underline{54} \\ 6 \text{ rows remaining which may be left at the top, or no decreases made} \end{array}$$

CHARTING A V-SHAPED NECKLINE

The front of a raglan pullover is worked the same as the back until the neck shaping. The V-shaped neck is the simplest neckline, and will be our first example.

The same number of stitches at the neck back are available and used for the neck front. The stitches are worked differently, however. We need 1 stitch at the top on each side of the V-shaped neck for a smooth line. There are 30 neck stitches altogether. Deduct the 1 stitch from each side for the fronts and 28 stitches remain—one half, or 14, to be decreased on one side and the other half, or 14, to be decreased on the other side. The depth of the V will determine how to place the 14 decreases. In our example we will plan a 7-inch V-neck depth, or 42 rows:

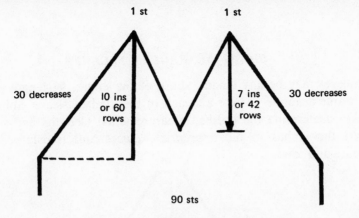

Fig. 129. Charting a V-shaped neckline

Determine the placement of the neck decreases by dividing the number of rows of the neck depth by the number of decreases to be made.

$$\begin{array}{r}\text{3 or every 3rd row a dec is made}\\\text{at each neck edge}\end{array}$$

14 dec. to be made $\quad\overline{\smash{)}\,42\ \text{rows—depth of V neck}}$

When you are working from the hem to the neck, you can determine the beginning of the neck shaping by deducting the number of rows of the neck depth from the total number of raglan rows:

$$\begin{array}{r}60\ \text{rows for raglan length}\\ -\ 42\ \text{rows for neck length}\\ \hline 18\ \text{rows from beginning of raglan shaping,}\end{array}$$

              or work 3 inches (translating rows back to inches) above beginning of raglan shaping, begin neck shaping.

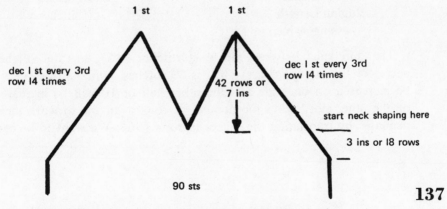

137

Fig. 130. Determining the beginning of the neck shaping

Sleeves may be any length: short, elbow-length, ¾-length or long, as in our example. Make a sketch of the kind of sleeve you plan to make. Determine the finished measurements, (lengths and widths), insert the inches in the appropriate places and translate them to stitches and rows:

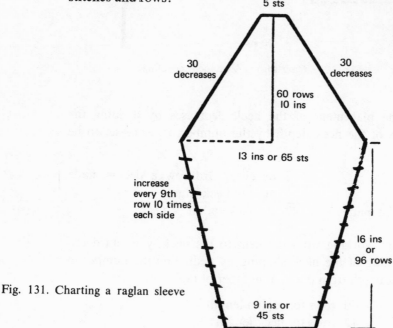

5 sts

30 decreases   30 decreases

60 rows
10 ins

13 ins or 65 sts

increase every 9th row 10 times each side

16 ins
or
96 rows

Fig. 131. Charting a raglan sleeve

9 ins or
45 sts

Wrist	9 inches
Upper Arm	13 inches
Sleeve Length	16 inches
Raglan Length (same as back)	10 inches

The difference between the wrist stitches (45) and the stitches necessary for the upper arm (65) is 20 stitches. One half or 10 will be increased on one side and the other half or 10 will be increased on the other side. Find the number of rows available to work these increases by translating the inches to rows (96). We want to be certain that the last increase is made at least 1 inch below the beginning of the raglan shaping, so deduct this 1 inch, or 6 rows, first. Ninety rows are then actually available to increase in. Divide the rows by the increases to be made.

	9	or every 9th row increase at the beginning and end of the row until 65 sts.
10 inc. to be made	90 rows	

The raglan is shaped the same as the back, 30 stitches decreased each side (60 stitches altogether). This leaves 5 stitches at the top of the sleeve which will become part of the neckline, when assembled.

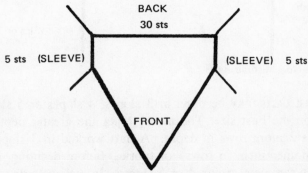

Fig. 132. How sleeves, back and fronts join for the neckline

In charting your own raglan sleeve, be certain that the number of stitches at the upper arm will allow you to make the same number of decreases as on your raglan back with at least a few stitches left at the top. There may be times when you will seem to have too many stitches at the upper arm to achieve this; but this will bring the sleeve in better proportion to the rest of the sweater.

ADDING BUSTLINE DARTS

To enhance the feminine shaping of a pullover, you may want to work in bust darts (see chapter 10). The bust darts allow you to have more rows or inches of fabric over the bustline, where it is needed,

139

without adding rows or inches to the side seams.

To determine the placement of the darts, draw a horizontal line from the bust to the side seam, then measure the length from this point to the beginning of the raglan shaping, and from this point to the hem. This will tell you how far to work before beginning the bust darts. Also measure the horizontal line to know how many stitches the dart should include.

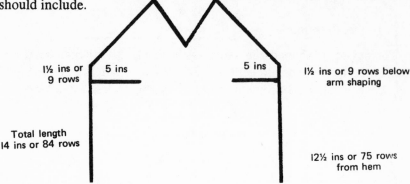

Fig. 133. Measuring for bustline darts

The bust darts may be done in 3 slopes, 4 slopes or 5 slopes, depending on the bust size. The more slopes the greater depth. Each slope adds 2 more rows in depth. A dart worked in 3 slopes would give us another inch (6 rows) of fabric. Before deciding, however,. work some samplers, trying 4 or 5 slopes. In our example we need a bust dart 5 ins. long, or over 25 sts, which may be divided according to the number of slopes we have decided on (fig. 133).

Fig. 134. Charting bustline darts according to fullness needed

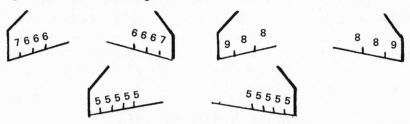

Rechart the raglan, using the same inches, but translated into a 6 st-7 row gauge.

Select a color, a yarn or yarn combination, a pattern stitch, a finish and a trim, and design your own V-neck raglan pullover.

A RAGLAN CARDIGAN

To make a cardigan, split the center front in half; back and sleeves are worked the same for a cardigan as for a pullover.

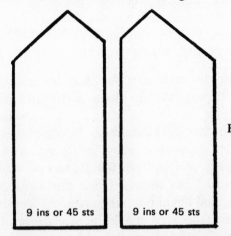

Fig. 135. Splitting the raglan for a cardigan

9 ins or 45 sts   9 ins or 45 sts

If the cardigan is to be buttoned, add stitches for a button overlap. If a double-breasted cardigan is desired, determine the width of the button overlap, translate to stitches and add to the cast on. In the example there is a 4-inch button overlap. To center the overlap add 2 inches of stitches to one side and 2 inches of stitches to the other side.

How to Decrease the Extra 10 Sts at the Neck

If you wish to maintain the same slope for the button overlap as for the V-shaped neck, which is decreased every third row, 30 rows, or 5 ins, would be needed to decrease 10 sts, or 72 rows from the beginning of the shaping to the top, and 72 rows from the hem, or 12 ins, or the extra sts may be bound off at once (fig. 136).

Fig. 136. Two ways of adding an overlap on a buttoned cardigan

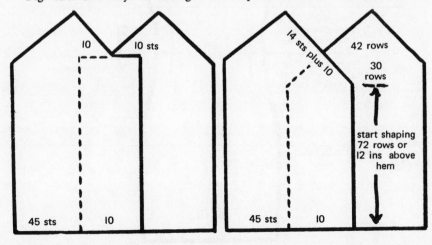

10   10 sts

45 sts   10

14 sts plus 10   42 rows

30 rows

start shaping
72 rows or
12 ins above
hem

45 sts   10

You now know how to make a raglan pullover and a raglan cardigan. Make the pullover long for a dress, incorporating the dress dart in Chapter 8, for shaping. You may make the cardigan long for a coat or coatdress, allowing for buttonholes. See the chapter on necklines for neckline variations.

CHARTING A DRESS WITH DARTS

In our example we will use the dress dart variation for a slight shaping. For a more fitted shaping, use the dress dart with lifted increase.

First determine how long the dress dart should be. In our example we will use a 10-inch dart. Then decide how many inches are needed at the waist for a subtle shaping. We will not use the actual waist measurement which is 26 inches, but instead make the waist 32 inches, or 4 inches less than the total hip or bust measurement. Decide, too, how far from the side seams the darts should be placed. In our example, we will place the darts 3 inches from each side seam. Shaping will be in the darts only, not at the sides. For details on side-shaping, see *Charting a Fitted One-Piece Dress*.

It is easier to figure the dart from the waist up first, then reverse it to chart it from the waist down.

Make a diagram first, insert the necessary inches, stitches and rows, and divide the rows by the stitches to be increased or decreased to determine the placement.

KNITTING A RAGLAN FROM THE NECK DOWN

Make a sketch of the previous raglan, fitting the different sections together. Insert the inches and stitches, changing decreases to increases and increases to decreases.

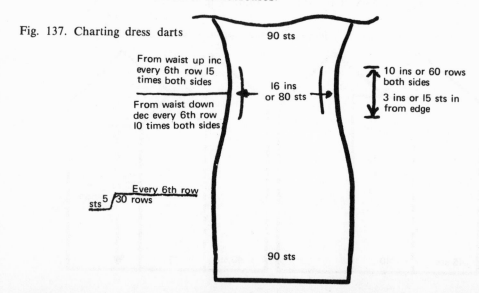

Fig. 137. Charting dress darts

90 sts

From waist up inc every 6th row 15 times both sides

From waist down dec every 6th row 10 times both sides

16 ins or 80 sts

10 ins or 60 rows both sides

3 ins or 15 sts in from edge

Every 6th row
sts 5 / 30 rows

90 sts

Fig. 138. Putting the raglan sections together to chart a one-piece raglan from the neck down

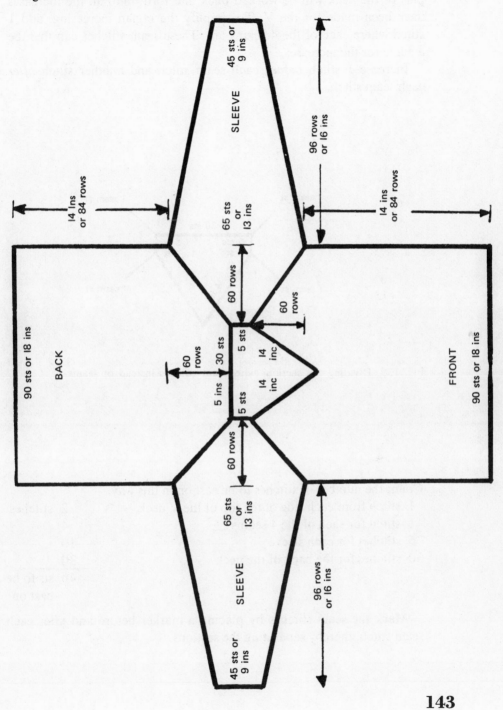

143

The stitches are cast on at the neck and, because it is a V neck, part of the neck will be worked back and forth until all the increases have been made for the V. To simplify the raglan increasing, add 1 stitch where each of the 4 seams are. These seam stitches can then be a guide for the increases.

Increase 1 stitch *before* each seam stitch and another stitch *after* each seam stitch.

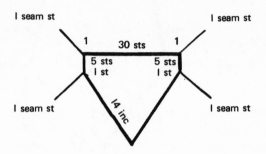

Fig. 139. Dividing the sections with seam stitches instead of seams

Count the number of stitches to be cast on in this way.

1 stitch from each side of the top of the V neck	2 stitches
1 stitch for each of the 4 seams	4
5 stitches for each sleeve	10
30 stitches for the back of the neck	30
	46 sts to be cast on

Mark the seam stitches by placing a marker before and after each seam stitch, thereby separating the sections.

144

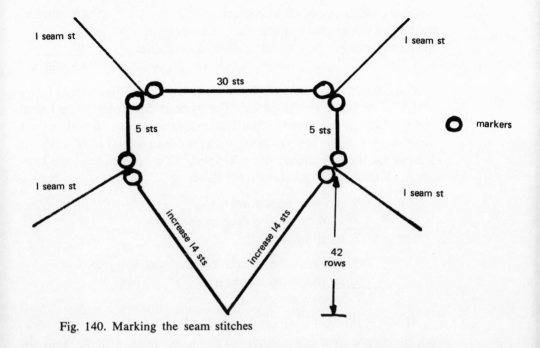

Fig. 140. Marking the seam stitches

Every other row there will be an increase before and after each seam stitch, and every 3rd row there will be an increase at the beginning and end of needle (V neck edge), 14 times. (See above.) At this point we will have worked 42 rows, or the depth of the V-shaped neck.

To find how many stitches there should be on the needle after working 42 rows, multiply the number of increase rows by the number of stitches increased on each row. Add the number of stitches cast on at the beginning, and the number of stitches increased at each neck edge, together with the seam stitch increases (see fig. 140):

You'll have increased 8 stitches every other row (1 stitch before and 1 stitch after each of the seam stitches). Altogether 42 rows are worked. Seam stitch increases were only worked on the knit rows, therefore, the number of increase rows is 21:

$$
\begin{array}{r}
21 \text{ increase rows} \\
\times \quad 8 \text{ stitches increased} \\
\hline
168 \text{ more stitches}
\end{array}
$$

145

number of stitches cast on at beginning	46 stitches
number of stitches increased at each seam, totaled	168
number of stitches increased at V-shaped neck edge	28
	242 stitches

You should then have 242 stitches on the needle when the V-shaped neck has been completed. The work is now ready to be joined and worked on the round. Continue increasing before and after each seam stitch every other row until you've worked a total of 60 rows, or 3 more inches (18 rows). At this point, 72 more stitches have been added (a total of 314 stitches on needle).

$$
\begin{array}{r}
9 \text{ more increase rows made} \\
\times \quad 8 \text{ sts increased on each increase row} \\
\hline
72 \text{ more stitches}
\end{array}
$$

$$
\begin{array}{r}
242 \text{ stitches were on needle when work was joined} \\
+ \quad 72 \text{ more stitches increased} \\
\hline
314 \text{ stitches altogether}
\end{array}
$$

At this point, you separate the sleeves from the front and the back; put the sleeve stitches on stitch-holders to be worked later. Work the back and front stitches (90 + 90) along with the 4 seam stitches, or 184 sts altogether, on the round until the length is reached (see fig. 141).

After you have completed body of pullover, work back and forth on the 65 sleeve sts, decreasing every 9th row 10 times (reversing the shaping of the sleeve of the raglan worked in sections). Bind off when sleeve measures 16 inches. Work the other sleeve in the same way.

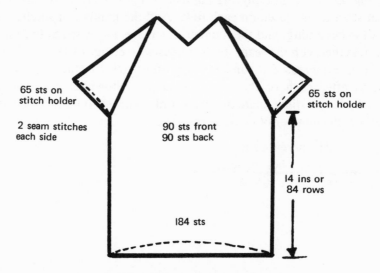

Fig. 141. Dividing the sections to work the remainder of the sleeves and body of the one-piece raglan

24 SET-IN SLEEVE: PULLOVERS, CARDIGANS AND DRESSES

New measurements needed, as shown in fig. 142, are:

Shoulder to Shoulder	15 inches
Armseye	18 inches
Depth of Cap	5½ inches

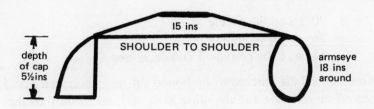

Fig. 142. How to determine measurements needed for a set-in-sleeve pullover

The beginning of either the set-in sleeve pullover (or the cardigan) is the same as the raglan (worked in sections), until you reach the underarm shaping. You determine the number of stitches bound off and decreased by the inches of stitches needed for the shoulders to fit

147

and decreased by the inches of stitches needed for the shoulders to fit well. To do this, measure from one shoulder tip straight across the back to the other shoulder tip. In our example this measurement is 15 inches, fig. 143.

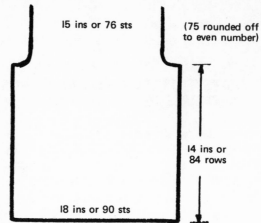

Fig. 143. Determining stitches needed for shoulder-to-shoulder measurement

This tells us that there are 14 stitches to be bound off and decreased at the underarms:

90 sts on the needle
− 76 sts for shoulders
14 sts to be bound off and decreased

One-half of the stitches to be bound off and decreased (or 7) are taken off on one side and the other half, or 7, taken off the other side. The stitches to be bound off and the stitches to be decreased are determined by taking half, or as close to half as possible, in a bind-off, and the remaining sts in decreases every other row or every K row.

In our example the extra stitch is added to the bind-off (fig. 144):

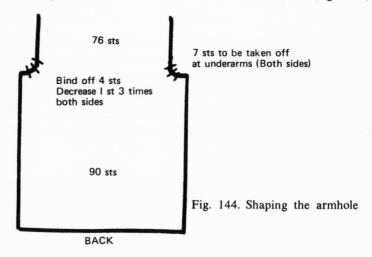

148

Fig. 144. Shaping the armhole

To know how far to work before beginning the shoulder shaping, we need to know the finished complete armhole measurement. In our example it is 18 inches.

Because we are charting the back only, half the armseye measurement, or 9 inches, is needed for the back. It is easier to measure in a straight line than around a curve, so we will deduct the curve by taking 1½ inches away from half the armseye measurement.

$$\begin{array}{rl} 9 & \text{inches—half of armhole measurement} \\ -\ 1\frac{1}{2} & \text{the curve} \\ \hline 7\frac{1}{2} & \text{inches straight up from beginning of underarm shaping,} \\ & \text{or 45 rows.} \end{array}$$

Seven and one-half inches, or 45 rows, are worked before beginning the shoulder shaping.

The set-in sleeve pullover front is the same as the back, until the neck shaping. If you wish a V-shaped neck, decrease half of the neck sts on one side of the V, and the other half on the other side of the V, as in the raglan, see fig. 145:

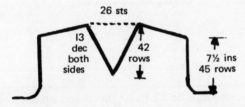

Fig. 145. Determining armhole length and fashioning a V-neckline

$$\begin{array}{rl} & \quad\quad 3 \ \text{or every third row} \\ \text{7-inch V-shaped neck depth and 13 decreases} & \underline{42 \ \text{rows}} \\ & \underline{39} \\ & 3 \ \text{rows left at the top} \end{array}$$

To make a shell or a sleeveless dress, the armseye measurement will be slightly smaller, so your slip does not show, and you may want to have the shoulder-to-shoulder measurement smaller. Think about using the bust dart. Select an edging, a stitch, a trim, and start designing. For a fitted shell or sleeveless dress, make a sketch first, determine the inches of stitches desired at the waist, and increase to the bustline.

Bust	36 inches
Waist	26 inches
Length from Waist to Underarm	8 inches

Determine the number of increases needed to go from the waist to the underarm by subtracting the waist stitches from the stitches needed at the bustline.

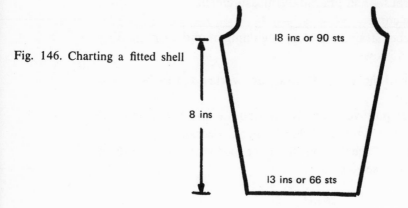

Fig. 146. Charting a fitted shell

18 ins or 90 sts

8 ins

13 ins or 66 sts

$$\begin{array}{r} 90 \\ -\ 66 \\ \hline \end{array}$$

24 sts, one half or 12 to be increased on each side.

Then determine the increase placement by first subtracting 1 inch from the total waist to underarm measurement so that the last increase will be made at least one inch below the beginning of the armhole shaping, then translate the inches into rows, and divide the rows by the number of increases to be made.

$$\begin{array}{r} 8\ \text{inches} \\ -\ 1\ \text{inch} \\ \hline \end{array}$$

7 inches actually available or 42 rows

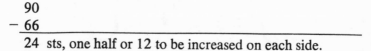

12 inc. $\begin{array}{r} 3 \\ \overline{42}\ \text{rows} \\ 36 \\ \hline \end{array}$

6 rows left or 1 inch

150

In other words, we would cast on 66 sts. Work 6 rows or 1 inch even, then increase 1 stitch each side every 3rd row until 90 stitches are on the needle, then work 1 more inch until 48 rows or 8 inches have been worked altogether.

CHARTING A FITTED ONE-PIECE DRESS

You may easily combine a fitted shell with a skirt to make a one-piece dress. Make a sketch first. Insert necessary widths and lengths, then translate to stitches and rows. Using the *Straight Skirt with Side Seams* and the *Fitted Shell* as an example, the following all-inclusive measurements are used:

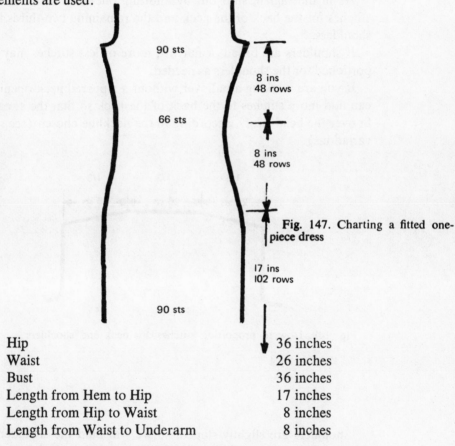

90 sts

8 ins
48 rows

66 sts

8 ins
48 rows

Fig. 147. Charting a fitted one-piece dress

17 ins
102 rows

90 sts

Hip	36 inches
Waist	26 inches
Bust	36 inches
Length from Hem to Hip	17 inches
Length from Hip to Waist	8 inches
Length from Waist to Underarm	8 inches

Only half the hip, waist and bust measurements are used in the diagrams, of course, as the dress is made in 2 pieces (see fig. 147).

The decreases and increases are the same in the one-piece dress as for just a skirt or a fitted shell. To finish the dress, shape the underarms as on pages 150 and 151; then see "How to Proportion Stitches for Neck and Shoulders" below. If sleeves are desired, see "Charting the Set-in Sleeve" below.

For a cardigan, split the front in half; add stitches for button overlap, if desired, as explained in the raglan example.

HOW TO PROPORTION STITCHES FOR THE NECK AND SHOULDERS

As in the raglan, start out by allotting one-third of the number of stitches for the back of the neck and the remaining two-thirds for both shoulders.

If shoulders are broad or narrow, more or less stitches may be proportioned for the shoulders as needed.

If you are working a pullover without a zippered neck opening, you can add more stitches to the back of the neck so that the sweater will fit over the head easily, according to the neckline chosen (see neckline variations).

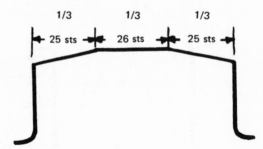

Fig. 148. How to proportion stitches for neck and shoulders

Shoulders are slightly sloped, so we will bind the shoulder stitches off in slopes. The shoulder bind-offs may be worked in 3, 4, or 5 slopes depending on the gauge and the slope desired. In this example, we will work the shoulder bind-offs in 3 slopes as shown in fig. 149. (See Short Row Bust Dart Sampler, with note on short-row shoulder bind-offs.) The 26 neck stitches may be bound off or put on a holder.

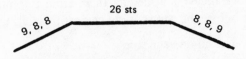

Fig. 149. Shaping shoulders

CHARTING THE SET-IN SLEEVE

This is handled in the same way as the raglan sleeve until you come to the shaping of the cap. Determine the depth of the cap and translate into rows. The bind-off and decreasing on the beginning of the sleeve cap are identical with those for the armholes on the back.

Allow approximately 2 inches of stitches at the top of the cap, to be bound off straight (may be 2-5 inches).

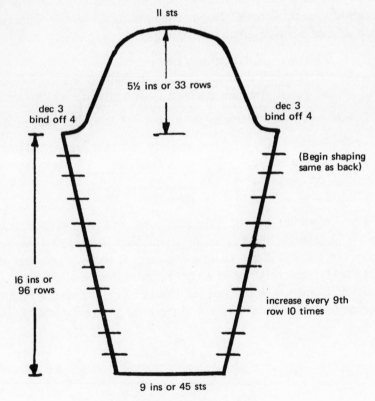

Fig. 150. Charting the set-in sleeve

The remaining stitches are decreased in the remaining rows of the depth of cap.

To determine how many stitches and how many rows remain and how to work the decreases, add the stitches accounted for (we know how to work them) and deduct them from the number of stitches on the needle before the cap shaping begins; this tells us what is left:

Stitches bound off on each side	8
Stitches decreased on each side	6
Stitches left at the top of cap	11
	25 sts accounted for

Stitches on needle before cap shaping begins	65 stitches
Stitches we know how to work	− 25 stitches
	40 stitches left

One half (or 20) will be decreased on one side and the other half (20) decreased on the other side.

Determine how many rows are available to work the decreases in by subtracting the number of rows used up in beginning the shaping of the cap from the total number of rows in the depth of cap. Each decrease uses up 2 rows. In our example there were 3 decreases on each side, or 6 rows used up (see fig. 151).

33 rows	Total depth of cap
− 6 rows	Taken up to begin cap shaping
27 rows	Remain available to decrease in

Divide the rows available by the number of decreases to be made.

	1	or every row (beg and end of knit
20 sts to be dec.	27 rows available	and purl rows)
on each side	20	
	7 rows left	

The 7 rows left we will make purl rows, rows we will not decrease on. Add them to the beginning of the cap shaping, by decreasing every *other* row 7 times (decreasing only at the beg and end of the knit rows), then *every* row as we get closer to the top of the cap.

To find out how many stitches should be on the needle before beginning to decrease *every* row, add the total number of stitches bound

154

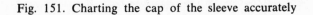

Fig. 151. Charting the cap of the sleeve accurately

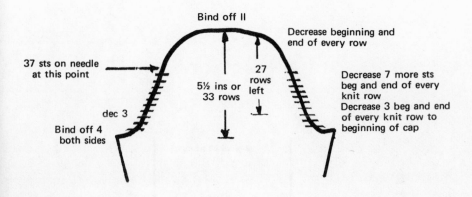

Bind off 11

Decrease beginning and
end of every row

37 sts on needle
at this point

27
rows
left

5½ ins or
33 rows

Decrease 7 more sts
beg and end of every
knit row
Decrease 3 beg and end
of every knit row to
beginning of cap

dec 3

Bind off 4
both sides

off and decreased at that point and subtract from the number of stitches on the needle to begin with.

Stitches bound off	8
Stitches dec. at beg. of shaping	6
Stitches dec. to continue shaping	14
	28 sts decreased
	at this point

    65 sts on needle before cap shaping begun
− 28 sts decreased
    37 sts should be on the needle before decreasing *every* row

Decrease at the beginning and end of every row until 11 sts remain. Bind off.

155

Work the drop-sleeve style by knitting the body straight (no arm-hole shaping), but marking for the armhole, and picking up the sleeve stitches after the shoulder seams have been assembled; then work the sleeve to the wrist (see fig. 152).

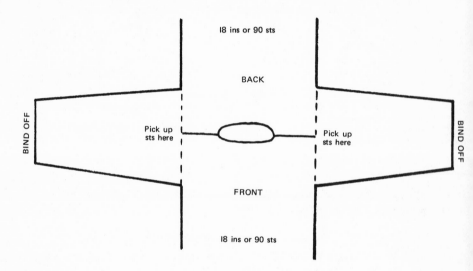

Fig. 152. Charting a drop-sleeve knit

The cap-sleeve, or dolman-sleeve style, is worked by casting on for the sleeve, and knitting it along with the body of the knit. Some of the sleeve sts may be increased and the remainder cast on, or they may all be cast on at one time (see fig. 153).

For long sleeves, cast on the number of stitches necessary to achieve desired length. Stitches may be bound off straight or in slopes at the shoulders, according to your design. In the above example, the shoulder bind-off was worked in four slopes.

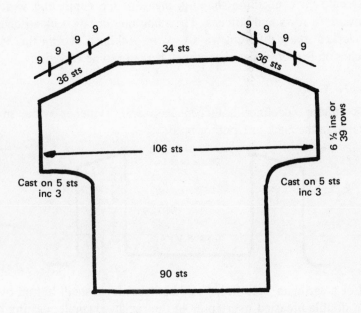

Fig. 153. Charting a cap-sleeve or dolman-sleeve knit

VARIED NECKLINE SHAPINGS

Decide on a neckline shaping, measure the depth and width and translate to rows and stitches. The same number of neck stitches may be worked many different ways to vary necklines. Using the 26 neck stitches on the set-in sleeve example, here are some variations.

Square Neck

A square neckline, 8 inches deep and 5 inches wide, may be squared in the back or front, or both:

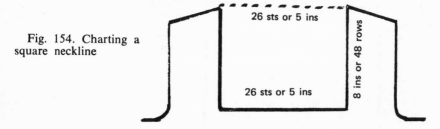

Fig. 154. Charting a square neckline

26 sts or 5 ins

26 sts or 5 ins

8 ins or 48 rows

For a cardigan, split in half, add stitches for a small button overlap, or a double-breasted overlap as in the raglan example, casting on the extra stitches at the bottom, and binding them off at the neckline; see fig. 155.

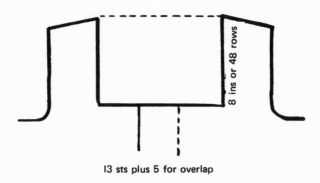

8 ins or 48 rows

13 sts plus 5 for overlap

Fig. 155. Charting a square neckline cardigan

U-shaped Neck

For a U-shaped neckline, 12 inches deep and 5 inches wide, work a decrease every knit row, or evenly in the 72 rows, according to your design. See fig. 156.

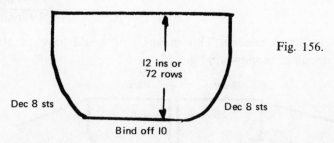

12 ins or
72 rows

Dec 8 sts

Dec 8 sts

Bind off 10

Fig. 156.

This neckline may be split for a cardigan.

Oval Neck

Figure 157 shows an oval neckline, 3 inches deep and 5 inches wide.

In making a pullover, you must be certain that the neck opening is large enough to fit over the head easily. If it is not large enough, leave an opening at the back of the neck and sew in a zipper, or work a row of single crochet, chain a small loop for a buttonhole, and button it.

One way to determine how large a neck opening should be, so as to fit over the head easily, is to measure the head and allow a few inches for the natural stretch of the knitted fabric. Use the oval neckline 3 inches deep and 5 inches wide as an example. You are making a pullover that needs to be put on over a head measuring 23 inches. How many inches will an oval neckline 3 inches deep and 5 inches wide give us?

Add the inches given for the back of the
neck   5 inches
The same number of inches are used for
the front   5 inches

159

Three inches of depth are given us on
    each side of neck   6 inches
The natural stretch of the knit will give
    us a few more   3 inches
                                               (approx.)
                                     19 inches

23 inches is needed. This means you would have to allow for a back opening, as shown in fig. 157.

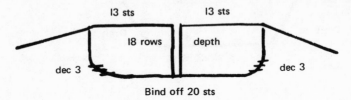

Fig. 157. Charting an oval neckline

If you do not want a back opening, you'll need 4 more inches of stitches for the sweater to fit over the head easily. You may get these additional 4 inches by taking 1 inch from each shoulder on the back, and 1 inch from each shoulder on the front.

Using your set-in sleeve cardigan as an example, add 1 inch or 5 stitches from each shoulder to the neck (see fig. 158).

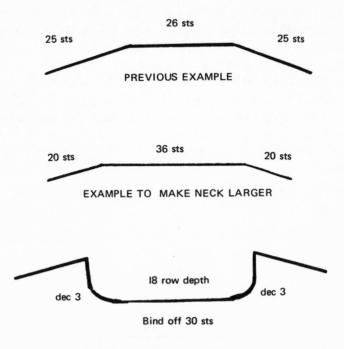

Fig. 158. Making a pullover neckline larger

A draped neckline:

Using the larger neck as an example, after the shoulder bind-off has been completed on the front, continue knitting 3 inches more, then bind off. Make a pleat and sew to the shoulder seam, and fold top down 1 inch and hem. Drape may be on back or front (see fig. 159):

Fig. 159. Charting a slightly draped neckline

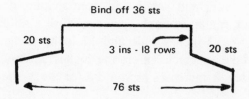

For a more luxurious drape, stitches may be increased as you approach the neckline. Use the lifted increase, and increase in a V formation (see fig. 160):

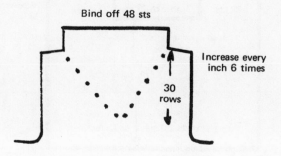

Fig. 160. Charting a more luxurious draped neckline

COLLARS

A Simple Turtleneck Collar

You can make this by picking up the neckline sts, and working a ribbing for the desired length, or you may wish to have an inch of ribbing around the neckline. (Use 1 or 2 sizes smaller needles.)

161

A Simple Collar

You work this one by picking up the neckline stitches, working a ribbing for 1 inch, then changing to a larger needle and working stockinette stitch until desired length. Many kinds of stitch combinations may be used here.

A Sailor Collar

Determine the width and length and front shaping desired. Using the V-shaped neck raglan example, you can work a sailor collar. The back is to measure 12 inches wide and 11 inches long and fit a V-shaped neck. Make a sketch, insert the inches and rows, and work the collar decreases or increases as you did for the V-shaped neck on the raglan.

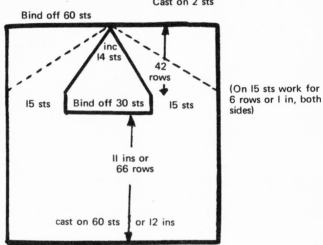

Fig. 161. Charting a sailor collar

To decrease to the point of the V, divide the number of rows available by the number of decreases to be made.

$$\begin{array}{r} 1 \ \text{or every row} \\ 30\overline{)42} \\ \underline{30} \\ 12 \ \text{rows} \end{array}$$

Work 12 of the 42 rows, then decrease every row.

162

The collar front may be bound off straight or be decreased to the point of the V. Determine rows and the number of decreases to be worked within those rows.

A Shawl Collar

This may be made by using the same raglan as an example, as shown in fig. 162.

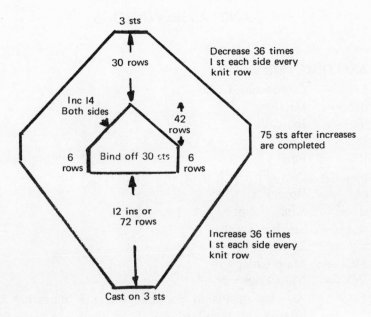

Fig. 162. Charting a shawl collar

When you plan a collar for a cardigan you may wish to add facings. See samplers 20 and 21.

Work a rolled collar by picking up the neckline stitches, working 3 inches, binding off loosely, folding in half, and hemming the bind-off to the inside of the neck. It's a good idea to use the picot hem here (sampler 19).

GLOSSARY OF TERMS
AND ABBREVIATIONS

KNITTING TERMS:

CC — Contrasting Color
dec — Decrease
inc — Increase
K — Knit
P — Purl
psso — Pass slip stitch over knit stitch
rnd — Round
sl — Slip, or slipped
st(s) — Stitch or stitches
tog — Together
MC — Main Color
YO — Yarn Over
* — Asterisk means to continue the row repeating from the asterisk, or between asterisks if there are asterisks at the beginning and end of a portion of instructions.

CROCHETING TERMS:

ch — Chain
hdc — Half Double Crochet
dc — Double Crochet
sc — Single Crochet
sl st — Crocheted chain through knitted or crocheted material.
sp — Space
trc — Treble Crochet

PART V:
SPECIAL
SUPPLEMENT

26 KNITTING WITH BIG NEEDLES

The very large needles (¾ to 1 inch in diameter) are great fun to work with and can be used to whip up a knit in hours. *Stitch Gauge:* It's particularly important to measure over several inches instead of just one inch when you use the large needles, because the tiniest fraction of an inch can make a tremendous difference in the finished measurement. Better measure as you work along, too, so as to be certain of the fit. You can use many of the pattern stitches in this book with the very large needles, and get a completely different effect. Experiment not only with different stitches but also with different yarn combinations. The large-needle knits are also a very good way to use up skeins of yarn of which only a small amount has been used. Unravel that knit you don't wear any more and remove the kinks by

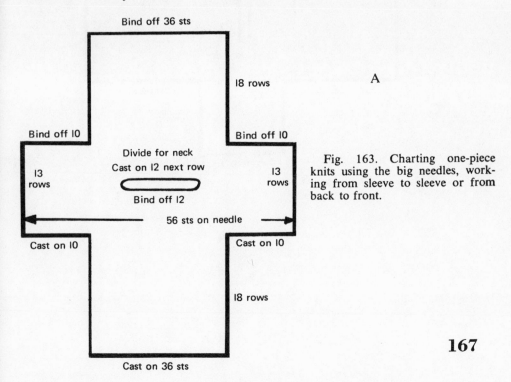

Fig. 163. Charting one-piece knits using the big needles, working from sleeve to sleeve or from back to front.

167

letting the yarn soak in cool water; rewind it and use it as one of the strands of yarn. Five or six strands of yarn may be used. Experiment with the number of strands you like best, too. The large-needle knits also give us the opportunity to plan knits with as few seams as possible, a challenge to the designer.

Example of a knit to be worked on the very large needles and made in one piece:

Gauge: 1 st—1 inch, 1 row—1 inch
Width: 36 inches
Length: 18 inches

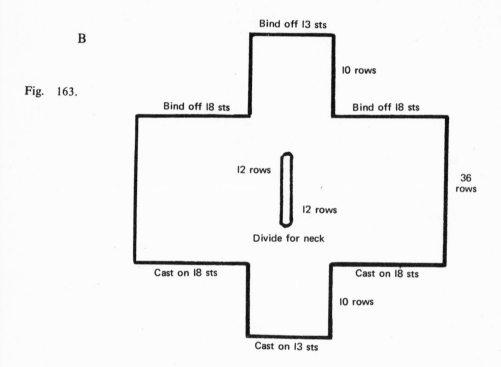

B

Fig. 163.

Bind off 13 sts

10 rows

Bind off 18 sts   Bind off 18 sts

12 rows

36
rows

12 rows

Divide for neck

Cast on 18 sts   Cast on 18 sts

10 rows

Cast on 13 sts

27 KNITTING ACCORDING TO A SEWING PATTERN

Purchase a pattern according to your measurements. In our example (fig. 164), an actual size-14 pants pattern is used. Our knitting gauge is 5 sts = 1 inch, and 6 rows = 1 inch. When you

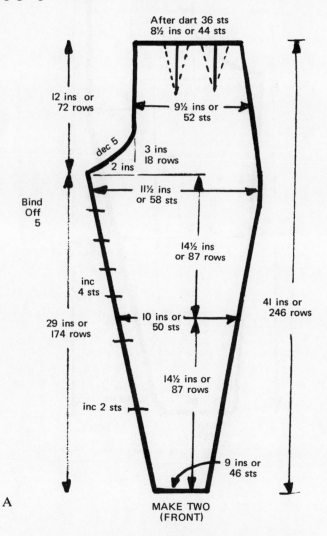

Fig. 164. Diagramming a pants sewing pattern

measure, eliminate hem and seam allowances. Add 2 sts for each seam. Make a diagram of the pants section. Insert the inches; inches are determined by measuring the pattern at the ankle, knee, thigh, width at crotch, hip and waist. Measure length from ankle to knee, to thigh, and then to crotch; and measure from crotch to waist. Translate these inches into stitches and rows. Round out the stitches to the next even number so there will be an even number of decreases. Measure length and width of darts.

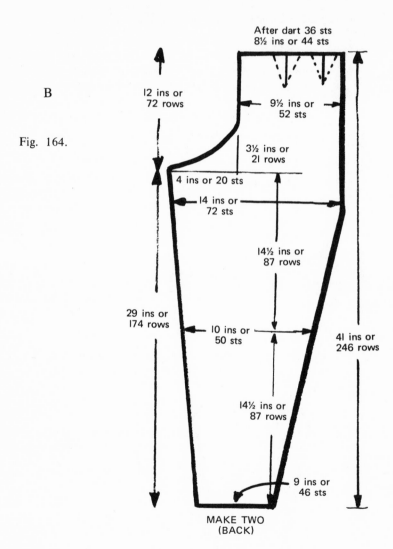

B

Fig. 164.

After dart 36 sts
8½ ins or 44 sts

12 ins or
72 rows

9½ ins or
52 sts

3½ ins or
21 rows

4 ins or 20 sts

14 ins or
72 sts

14½ ins or
87 rows

29 ins or
174 rows

10 ins or
50 sts

41 ins or
246 rows

14½ ins or
87 rows

9 ins or
46 sts

MAKE TWO
(BACK)

170

DARTS

In the example (fig. 165), each dart is 3½ inches deep and eliminates ¾ inch from the waistline.

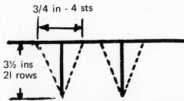

Fig. 165. Charting darts from a pants sewing pattern

Translate the inches into rows and sts; in this example, 4 sts should be decreased in 20 rows. Divide the rows by the sts:

$$\frac{5}{4}\quad\frac{\text{or every 5th row K 2 sts together}}{20\ \text{rows}}$$

When you can't decide exactly (as in this dart example) whether to decrease 3 or 4 sts, choose the number of sts which seems most likely to give you the best fit.

You may work the darts in the same places as the sewing pattern indicates.

CROTCH SHAPING

Measure the inches taken off and the inches used in doing it; translate to stitches and rows. You may bind off half and decrease half. This will vary.

Working section by section, determine the necessary increases, divide in half, determine the rows available and divide the rows by the number of increases. This indicates how to place the increases evenly. See first pants example.

Fig. 166. Shaping the crotch

171

PART VI:
DESIGNER'S
BOUTIQUE

Fig. 167. Design a pants and top with a high-fashion look. Shown here is an outfit using the basket-weave stitch (sampler 46, p. 71) and a crocheted loop trim (sampler 79, p. 99).

Fig. 168. A mock plaid skirt and cape, with a turtleneck pullover.
The spider stitch buttons (sampler 90, p. 105) are used on the
cape, and the skirt is straight with side seams. The mock plaid
(sampler 58, p. 81) is a very good way to combine colors.

Fig. 169. A dress with a cape collar (p. 163) worked on the very large needles, combining the stockinette stitch (sampler 3, p. 31) and garter stitch (sampler 1, p. 30) in squares, and edged with a single crochet (sampler 6, p. 34).

Fig. 170. Pants (using a pants sewing pattern, pp. 169-170) with a French cable trim (sampler 41, p. 66) and a shell top with a draped neckline (p. 161) that repeats the French cable trim.

Fig. 171. Make a poncho (p. 130) on the big needles (p. 167) with several strands of yarn. Cast on 2 stitches and increase to desired width. Add a bias trim (sampler 66, p. 90) worked on smaller needles and a tassel as shown here.

178

Fig. 172. Design a two-color outfit, with a full-fashioned (sampler 11, p. 41) short sleeved raglan cardigan (pp. 133, 141) with a wide stripe (sampler 51, p. 75) and a picot hem trim (sampler 19, p. 48). Make it long for a dress, or as shown here, make a two-piece, with the skirt matching one of the colors in the cardigan. Select the buttonhole technique and button you like best from instructions in the book.

Fig. 173. Beautiful original designs can be created just by combining stitches. Combine a popcorn (samplers 42-44, p. 68)) with a lacy cable (sampler 40, p. 66) and work it into the bodice of a day dress as shown here.

Fig. 174. A straight skirt, knitted circular-style (p. 127), and a shell top with a shawl collar (p. 163) trimmed with the reverse bell pattern (sampler 70, p. 93). The shawl collar shows the purl side as the right side.

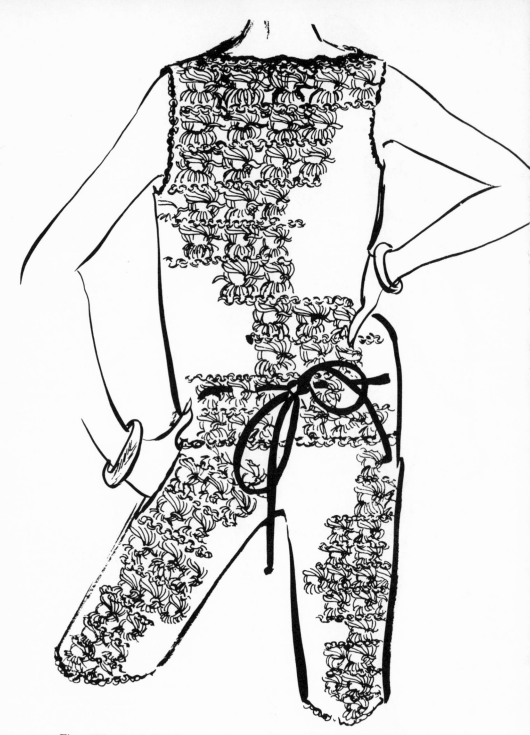

Fig. 175. A shell with knee-length pants worked in a knitted stitch with a crochet look and tied with a belt made in a knitted tubing (sampler 63, p. 89).

Fig. 176. A raglan pullover (p. 133) using the full-fashioned decreases (sampler 11, p. 41) and a bell-shaped sleeve (decrease from the cuff to the underarm instead of increase). The trim shown is a diamond pattern you can work out yourself (see leaf stitch, sampler 50, p. 73), or use any stitch to accent the collar, sleeves and hip.

Fig. 177. A short A-line dress with a set-in sleeve (p. 153), trimmed in the crocheted rickrack trim (sampler 77, p. 98) and tied with a velvet ribbon just under the bust.

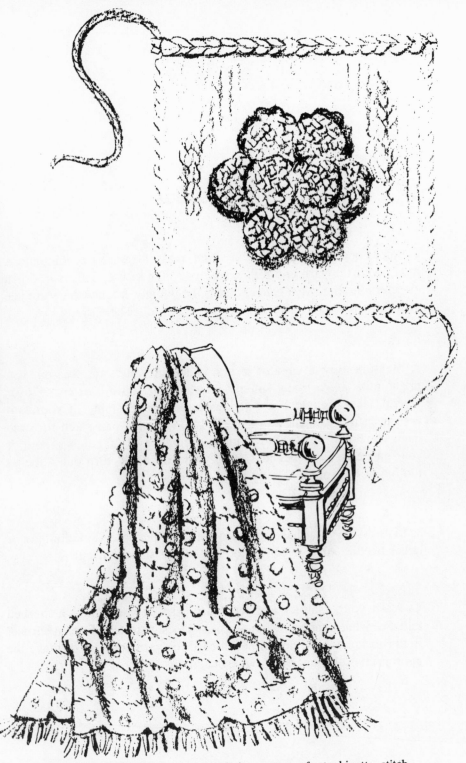

Fig. 178. Making an afghan: knit squares of stockinette stitch (sampler 3, p. 31) with popcorn stitch (samplers 42-44, p. 68) clusters in the center; sew them together, add some fringe (sampler 65, p. 89) and you have a lovely handcrafted gift.

STITCH GAUGE

1. Before beginning a knit of any kind, make a sampler of the pattern stitch, with the yarn and size needle you plan to use. This is in order to determine the *stitch gauge,* that is, how many stitches there are per inch. Stitches make inches, so this is essential. Therefore:

2. Measure over an area of several inches, not just one. Reason: you might miss a fractional difference which, if it were extended over several inches, could cause serious error. For example, if your knit is to measure 40 inches around, and you're off a half-stitch for each inch, you'll end up with an ultimate difference of 20 stitches. And, if your gauge is 5 stitches to 1 inch, your knit could turn out 4 inches too big or too small. Slightly fatal.

3. Let's assume you have too many stitches per inch. Solution: use a larger needle. And, if you've too few, use a smaller needle.

4. Wash your sampler and let it dry, just as you would a finished knit. See what happens. Is it colorfast? Does it stretch? Does it shrink? Better to know now, and either discard the yarn entirely, or make the appropriate allowance in your calculations.

STITCH GAUGE CHART

Example: If 20" of stitches are required and the stitch gauge is 4 stitches per inch, find the 4 column and follow it down to the 20" line to find the answer (80 stitches). It's simple arithmetic. This works for rows as well as stitches.

	stitches per inch						
	2½	3	3½	4	4½	5	5½
1½"	3-3/4	4½	5¼	6	6-3/4	7½	8¼
2"	5	6	7	8	9	10	11
2½"	6¼	7½	8-3/4	10	11¼	12½	13-3/4
3"	7½	9	10½	12	13½	15	16½
3½"	8-3/4	10½	12¼	14	15-3/4	17½	19¼
4"	10	12	14	16	18	20	22
4½"	11¼	13½	15-3/4	18	20¼	22½	24-3/4
5"	12½	15	17½	20	22½	25	27½
5½"	13-3/4	16½	19¼	22	24-3/4	27½	30¼
6"	15	18	21	24	27	30	33
6½"	16¼	19½	22-3/4	26	29¼	32½	35-3/4
7"	17½	21	24½	28	31½	35	38½
7½"	18-3/4	22½	26¼	30	33-3/4	37½	41¼
8"	20	24	28	32	36	40	44
8½"	21¼	25½	29-3/4	34	38¼	42½	46-3/4
9"	22½	27	31½	36	40½	45	49½
9½"	23-3/4	28½	33¼	38	42-3/4	47½	52¼
10"	25	30	35	40	45	50	55
10½"	26¼	31½	36-3/4	42	47¼	52½	57-3/4
11"	27½	33	38½	44	49½	55	60½
11½"	28-3/4	34½	40¼	46	51-3/4	57½	63¼
12"	30	36	42	48	54	60	66
12½"	31¼	37½	43-3/4	50	56¼	62½	68-3/4
13"	32½	39	45½	52	58½	65	71½
13½"	33-3/4	40½	47¼	54	60-3/4	67½	74¼
14"	35	42	49	56	63	70	77
14½"	36¼	43½	50-3/4	58	65¼	72½	79-3/4
15"	37½	45	52½	60	67½	75	82½
15½"	38-3/4	46½	54¼	62	69-3/4	77½	85¼

16"	40	48	56	64	72	80	88
16½"	41¼	49½	57-3/4	66	74¼	82½	90-3/4
17"	42½	51	59½	68	76½	85	93½
17½"	43-3/4	52½	61¼	70	78-3/4	87½	96¼
18"	45	54	63	72	81	90	99
18½"	46¼	55½	64-3/4	74	83¼	92½	101-3/4
19"	47½	57	66½	76	85½	95	104½
20"	50	60	70	80	90	100	110
25"	62½	75	87½	100	112½	125	137½
30"	75	90	105	120	135	150	165
40"	100	120	140	160	180	200	220

190

191